WORLD WITHOUT END

Religious Books in the Fontana Series

World Without End

ROGER PILKINGTON

COLLINS

fontana books

First Published by Macmillan & Co. 1960
First Issued in Fontana Books 1961

CONTENTS

INTRODUCTION

Opinions are never entirely one's own. A person may think that his judgment of a painting, a view across the rolling countryside of the English midlands, the melody of the willow-warbler or the political pronouncements of a statesman, are based only upon his private observation or reason; but this is not altogether true. He may well be right in thinking that his interpretation is in some special way his own, yet inevitably the basis on which he forms his opinion is to some extent derived from others. His background, the nature of his work, the views of his friends, the climate of opinion in the society in which he lives, and the great stream of traditional thought and knowledge inherent in his education—all these and more will play their part in developing his attitude to things as diverse as the reform of divorce laws and the works of a modern sculptor. Particularly is this the case in the matter of religious belief. Doctrine and dogma may be accepted, or modified, or even rejected; but the beliefs of others will undoubtedly have a profound influence in determining the detailed expression of the personal faith of the individual.

For this reason I cannot pretend that even such limited understanding of religious truths as I may possess is all my own work, and I am acutely conscious of the debt I owe to those who first introduced me to ideas and beliefs which I had later to consider as objectively as I was able, testing the lessons of childhood against the experience of later life. Besides, I am no theologian, and for that reason alone a number of truths may have passed me by without my comprehending them—just as the minor genetic abnormalities of the fruit-flies upon which I used to work might have gone unnoticed by a professor of Old Testament history. So if the reader should find in the course of this book that certain views are sometimes expressed with which he is inclined to agree, I hope that he will not impute to me any unusual insight. It is infinitely more probable that the credit belongs to some unknown friend of my earlier years, or to a teacher, or perhaps to the minister of a local church who may first have sown the seed of a train of thought which was to grow as the years went by. But if, on the other hand, I should express opinions which appear fundamentally unsound, then this is not necessarily the fault of those same influences. It is more likely to be attributable to the flights of my own fancy, or to that peculiar spiritual blindness to which, I believe, all of us are subject.

There are hundreds of millions of Christians scattered throughout the length and breadth of the world, and yet the faith of each one of them is to some extent a personal matter, differing in detail from that of all his fellows. In this book I have endeavoured to set down some of the conclusions to which I myself have come, but in so doing I have been only too well aware that many of the matters which I discuss have exercised the minds of philosophers and theologians for centuries. It would have been possible for me to draw on the writings of authors from the early fathers to C. S. Lewis or C. H. Dodd, but to do so would have taken me outside the scope of my purpose. Religious belief is not a matter of academics so much as of individual groping after truth, and of experience in one's own unique and quite individual life. I have therefore not concerned myself with the expert meditations of others, but only with the way in which certain aspects of faith present themselves to me as challenges to be met, or as problems to be faced.

For some, no problem may exist at the same points where I have found doubts or questionings, but I have reason to believe that many who grow up, as I have done, within the framework of a fundamentally scientific training may find themselves faced with much the same challenges to their thinking and to their faith as those which have at times confronted myself. And if so, then I cannot guarantee to provide all the answers, but only to point certain paths of thought along which perhaps a clearer understanding may lie.

I

FACING THE TRUTH

When ministers tell their congregations that the prime requirement of the Christian is to have faith as a little child, I am uneasy. If by " faith " one means simple and unquestioning trust, rather than a system of belief, then of course they are right. From the days of the New Testament onwards it has been true enough that a child-like trust has worked wonders, and there will always be those fortunate people who can obey a simple demand for unquestioning committal such as was made by Dr. Billy Graham at his massed gatherings in Harringay Arena, and who can apparently overcome in one simple bound all the problems of modern science and discovery. Overcome them—or perhaps ignore them. But others, because of temperament or upbringing, are not so fortunate. They demand that the system of beliefs which they are to hold must involve something more complex. To them, " faith " is not the unquestioning trust of an infant for its parent, but is more in the nature of understanding. If they are to hold a belief, then that belief must be in harmony with their experience, or at least it must not be contradicted by reason.

This is why the " faith as a little child " admonition, however true in one sense, seems to me to be so easily capable of misinterpretation. It almost suggests that Christianity itself is so simple that even an infant could in a moment *understand* its implications, whereas the beliefs of a Christian are really more complex and more demanding of intellectual exercise than any other facts or theories of any kind whatsoever. Atomic physics is no easy subject, and to grasp the theories of orbit jumps and quanta, of soft radiations and half-life and transitional elements, is difficult enough, but compared with the tenets of Christianity modern physical theory is simple indeed.

I doubt if this is sufficiently realised. Certainly it is
not often said, perhaps because Christians are so anxious
to portray their belief as something freely offered to all
men—as indeed it is. But a moment's consideration will
show that Christianity involves a great number of separate
beliefs, each of which is vital. For instance, one must
accept that there is an active creator, that the historical
Jesus was real, that the resurrection, the efficacy of prayer,
the reality of an ultimate good and evil are beyond doubt.
One must comprehend something of " redemption," of the
" power of the Holy Spirit " in human affairs, and one must
honestly believe that the Church is in quite a different
category from a debating society or a bowling club. These
are only a few of the basic tenets and doctrines, but refusal
to accept any one of them will debar an individual from
the Christian faith—not on any instructions of an ecclesiastical hierarchy, but in much the same way that it would be
impossible to live and work as a research physicist if one
believed mathematics to be sheer nonsense or refused to
accept the notions of nuclear fission and fusion.

Our distant forefathers were in one respect fortunate—
as some people still are, even to-day—in that they were
able to accept these things without much difficulty. It may
not have been possible to formulate a full and satisfactory
account of the creation or of how a moral law came to
pervade the universe, but at least there was no highly
developed system of learning which was continually unearthing fresh facts which seemed to point in the opposite
direction. In our own day, however, the situation is very
different. We live and move and have our being in a world
in which the astonishing and brilliant development of
scientific knowledge is perpetually presenting us with well-
tried and proven facts which are not primarily concerned
with religion at all, but which nevertheless offer a stern
challenge to some of the beliefs which we would like to be
able to hold.

Most of the theories of modern science are based on
abundant evidence, and whether or not they shock our

complacency they have to be accepted as true. Or perhaps
I should say that they can only be rejected as untrue if one
is willing to deceive oneself. Some people are of course
prepared to do so. If the Old Testament says that the
Earth is flat, then it *is* flat, they say, and there is nothing to
discuss. Magellan sailed round it? On the contrary, he
thought he sailed round it, they will assure themselves, but
in reality he was only navigating the circumference of a
wide circle on a flat plate. Fossils suggest that living
creatures have evolved from earlier types, far back in the
millions of bygone centuries? Nonsense! they declare.
And as for looking at the evidence, they would much prefer
not to do so.

I must admit to a trace of admiration for those who adopt
a rigidly fundamentalist attitude. They know what they
believe, and nothing will shake them. Far from being reeds
shaken by the wind, they would stand motionless in a
tornado. Such people have done great things in the history
of the Church, and if they write abusive postcards (as some
of them do) to persons like myself who do not regard
Genesis I as an infallible textbook of geophysics, then I
respect their fearless determination to fight to preserve what
they believe to be the revealed truth, against all comers.
And yet I hope they will forgive me (which is most
unlikely) if I say that on balance they are doing their cause
a disservice, and further, that I have a feeling that they
are being dishonest with others and with themselves. To
react to truth of any kind by refusing to admit its validity
is surely not very creditable, and to counter each new piece
of careful scientific research merely with a determination
not to accept it is not, I think, worthy of the human intellect.
A Melanesian islander whose first contact with the outside
world is by way of the strange things he may be taught by
a visiting Seventh Day Adventist can be forgiven for his
rigidity of outlook, but it is difficult to excuse students in
western universities and colleges who inherit the benefits
of science and yet refuse to face up to its findings. Fundamentalism in an educated person is, I suspect, very often a

cloak for intellectual cowardice; but however that may be, it is an attitude towards modern knowledge which many are bound to find unsatisfactory.

There is another way of countering scientific discovery which, though not dishonest, is at least unwise. This is to seize upon present gaps in the scientific scheme of things and to earmark them as areas in which the special creative activity of God can be permitted to operate. It seems reasonable to believe that some of the gaps in our knowledge may indeed be the result of our searching in vain for physical causes which in fact do not exist, but to allege special divine action as the operative agent whenever scientists cannot at the moment provide a complete explanation is far from wise. Yet this is often done. " Evolution? Ah, but what about the Missing Link? They'll never trace man back to the apes, you just mark my words. No, they'll never find the Missing Link. And why not? I'll tell you why not. Because it's not there to be found. *That's where God comes in, see?*"

How familiar this argument is, and how foolish. In Darwin's day the chain of evolution was so riddled with missing links that it was hardly a chain at all, yet one by one the gaps have been filled, and if any remain it is probably only because the requirements of oil-drilling and mining, or the construction of railways, have not at present led to excavations in those particular areas of the world where the remains of the stop-gaps might be found. But as the bulldozers march relentlessly forward, so more and more evidence comes to light, and one after another the little outposts of divine intervention hastily fortified by well-meaning Christians have to be abandoned.

" They won't split the atom. You can't unmake what God has made "—but to-day transmuted atoms if not actually ten a penny are at least ten for a thousand pounds. " It's not gravity, it's God that keeps the planets in their courses. Man will never be able to conquer space "—yet with a puff and a roar of flame from the launching-pads at Cape Canaveral and on the Russian steppes the man-made moons take flight to their orbits with astonishing accuracy.

Species, once regarded as sacrosanct specimens of the creator's handiwork, are no longer immutable. The difference between two distinct species of the fruit-fly has been traced to a different arrangement of the chromosomes, and by X-ray bombardment of the reproductive cells it has been possible to re-create one of the species artificially from the other.

The person who takes the natural and tempting course of appropriating on behalf of God the unsolved problems of life or the universe may be sincere, but he is guilty of a strategic error. Forced back on an ever-decreasing perimeter of defence, he is eventually left with no room to manœuvre, and no status for his God except as a rather inferior juggler most of whose tricks have already been detected. But more than this, the notion itself seems to me to be fundamentally unsound. It suggests that our world, and indeed the whole universe, is governed by two quite separate processes : on the one hand, the inexorable laws of a blind and soulless nature, and, on the other, the occasional capricious intervention of a God whose creative activity is at best confined to tying up the loose ends, and at worst to mere conjuring tricks. Such a God is hardly worthy of unqualified devotion, and certainly not of love. A God who can fairly command respect as a creator is neither an ingenious mechanic who wound up the clockwork some billions of years ago and then stood back to watch the machinery run down through the increasing entropy of the laws of thermodynamics, nor is he a God who acts on cosmic bank holidays and early closing days alone. The Christian asserts that God actually *sustains* the whole of creation, and by whatever means he may act (as, for instance, through the labour of dedicated men and women) he is as fully engaged in his creative activity *at this very moment* as he was in the remote geological past.

For myself, neither fundamentalism nor special intervention provides an adequate means of finding a unity between the works of God and the discoveries of science, since the one is an affront to the intellect and the other leads to an inadequate concept of the power of God. Two other courses remain open, and the first of these is to wave the wand of atheism and cause the difficulties to disappear by the simple expedient of denying God, or declaring that the question of his existence and attributes is irrelevant. It hardly needs to be pointed out that this is nothing more than inverted fundamentalism, and just as much of an affront to the intelligence. It is a spectacle ridiculous enough when some amiable member of a church flatly declines even to consider the evidence for evolution, dismissing the patient work of thousands of skilled and highly qualified biologists with the blithe remark that he doesn't care what they say, he just knows they must be wrong; but it is no less depressing a revelation of human folly when an astro-physicist or a biologist declares himself to be an atheist or an agnostic, without having so much as turned a page of any one of the thousands of books in which experts of a different faculty (theology) have carefully set down their experiences after a lifetime of study.

If a fundamentalist were to say to me that he had carefully studied the whole of the evidence from Wallace and Darwin to Morgan and the modern geneticists, and could find nothing at all to indicate that evolution had taken place, or that species were anything but constant and immutable, or even that the world was more than six thousand years old, then I would perhaps be surprised; but at least I would respect him and ask him to tell me more. And similarly, if a non-theologian were to inform me that he was thoroughly familiar with the original manuscripts of the Bible, had mastered the whole of biblical criticism from the Reformation onwards, had studied the writings of Aquinas and St. Thérèse of Lisieux, of William Temple and St. Paul and a hundred others, and could find nothing whatsoever in them which hinted at the possibility of a real communion between God and man, then again I would be impressed. But very often the denial is made from a position of quite unabashed ignorance, and it can surely be a reflection of nothing other than foolishness or conceit if a person makes pronouncements on extremely difficult and complex matters without so much as being willing to consider the findings of those who have spent a lifetime of research upon the same subject.

The final possibility is to consider what is the precise nature of scientific findings. It is clearly the case that science has particular methods of its own, and that it is mainly confined to investigating certain types of phenomena; yet there can be no doubt at all that science represents a view of a limited but nevertheless extensive field of reality. To say that science is not true is just nonsense. If the word "truth" has any validity at all, then *science is telling us the truth*. That is not to say that every scientific theory is correct, or that every hypothesis is valid and unchangeable for all time. Clearly this is not the case—even Newton is now known to have provided an erroneous if useful system of scientific laws—but it can hardly be denied that the discoveries of science are substantially correct, and that any closer approximation to complete reliability of statement usually comes in the form of greater accuracy of observation and measurement rather than in complete revision. Many theories may well be empirical, but by and large a discovery made and checked according to the traditions of science is as true as any statement can be.

Christians believe that their God is a "God of *truth* and love," and they repeat these words without hesitation. And if they regard truth as being of God—which is what they thus affirm—then it is difficult to see how science can properly be regarded as anything but a revelation of part of the divine scheme of things. To oppose the misuse of scientific knowledge (as in brain-washing) is one thing, but to regard each increase in our knowledge of nature and the universe as evil is quite another, and I believe that the proper attitude of the Christian should be to accept scientific discoveries, to try to understand them, and to face the challenge of attempting to integrate them with the certainty which he has received from other quite different sources. Only thus can he achieve the possession of a religious faith which does not involve a certain degree of sacrifice of his intellectual integrity.

I do not mean by this that everything connected with a

personal faith should be of such a nature that it is amenable to scientific analysis, but just that one should be confident that truth itself is not a thing of which to be afraid, from whatever source it may come. There are no doubt some who would disagree, pointing out that religious insight is not achieved through reason but by committal and dedication, and through awareness of a kind quite different from that of the scientist. And this of course is true enough. But I myself could never hold a belief in direct opposition to experienced truth, and in this inability I suspect that I am a not untypical product of the age of scientific education.

Science, then, can be regarded as a means of knowledge which inevitably involves at least a partial revelation of ultimate and divine truth. And yet it would be a mistake to imagine that by adopting this particular attitude the difficulties are at once overcome. On the contrary, they are accentuated, for many facets of Christian belief are ones upon which science will impinge. Sometimes advances in science will be of immediate help, at others irrelevant, but often they will present a challenge, and the findings of the laboratory will seem to conflict with firmly established belief.

The integration of science with personal faith is not easy. The fundamentalist has a much easier time of it, and so has the atheist. Both can close their eyes and stop their ears—and even gnash their teeth if they feel so inclined. But I think that the vision which is theirs may perhaps not be so bright as that of the person who can face truth unafraid, but in honest and inquiring humility.

II

SCIENTIFIC FAITH

People have a strange habit of regarding various kinds of experts in quite different lights. For instance, a county cricketer or an amiable and popular person with no specialised knowledge outside his own skill may broadcast over the radio on the subject of grace, or redemption, or the atonement, each of which is such a difficult concept that few would even venture a definition of the words themselves. The reaction of his hearers is generally that what he says must be true, not because he is a specialist in theology but *because he is not*. Yet if the same statements are made by a Regius Professor of Divinity at Cambridge, or by a leading bishop, then the common reaction is either that he is saying these things because he is paid to do so, or that he is biased, or that one need not believe what he says because he is talking on his own subject! This is no new trend of our own day. Robert Boyle, the great scientist of the seventeenth century, was the author of a number of theological works which were widely acclaimed, and he was urged to enter the Church, where a bishopric would quickly be made available for him. Yet he declined the offer, stating that his opinions carried weight because he was a layman, whereas if he were to preach the same things from within the priesthood people would merely say that he was paid to do so, and would not believe what he said. Strange though this common reaction is, I can at least take some comfort from it, for there will no doubt be some who will read this book with interest because it is written by a layman, whereas if the same matters were discussed more ably and authoritatively by a theologian they would not bother to take it off a library shelf.

I do not mean by this that theologians alone ought to command a hearing on the subject of religion, for religion to all and not to the specialist. A kennelman a tramp, or a geneticist or concert pianist have just as much right to a respectful hearing when they are telling us what religion means to them personally, but where it comes to the interpretation of doctrine or to biblical criticism and Church history then the views of the specialist are probably worth far more. God may certainly be apprehended by all, but some of his workings need extremely careful and critical study.

Yet although a layman may be credited with disinterested reliability on such a difficult subject as grace, the position in respect to science is very different. It is most unlikely that a county cricketer would ever be given a quarter of an hour or even a minute of broadcasting time to speak on radiation sickness or the formation of depressions in the Atlantic weather system, or the long-term effects upon cereal crops of changes in the level of the water-table. He might indeed have made one of these subjects his main interest as an amateur, but the reaction of the audience would certainly be that what he said was probably ill-informed. It would have been better to leave any such matters to a specialist, they would think, to a man who would know what he was talking about because he had studied the subject all his life, and who could be regarded as reliable because he held a professorial chair or a research fellowship *in which he was paid* to know about such things.

Perhaps this difference in the respect accorded to experts in different specialities is in part due to the notion that science is not only highly complex but is in essence truth of a rather superior kind. A scientific statement of fact is often regarded as thoroughly objective truth, based on dispassionate and careful observations which are exhaustively checked by experiment and do not rest on any emotional presuppositions or blind beliefs; whereas Church teaching is little more than a kind of wishful thinking based on a mass of unchecked and often unreasonable presuppositions. For example, the concept of the " forgiveness of sins," which is an item in the creed, must rest on the assumption that there is such a thing as sin, and, furthermore, that there is indeed a God who can forgive them—neither of which is demonstrable in the ordinary sense of the word. Yet to imagine that scientists work without presuppositions, and without any element of childlike faith, is the most extraordinary error.

One of Mendel's "Laws" of heredity states that if an individual with a dominant trait is crossed with one having the corresponding recessive trait, then all the first generation progeny will be phenotypically (*i.e.* in appearance) of the dominant type. But if these progeny are crossed among themselves, the next generation will show the original dominant and recessive characteristics in the proportion of 3 to 1. Now any person who conducts an experiment of this kind will find that 3 to 1 is *more or less* the answer he gets. If on a Wednesday afternoon he sows 1000 second generation sweet pea seeds from a suitable cross he may perhaps find that 746 yield tall plants and 254 yield small ones. He may repeat the experiment one Friday, and this time the result is 753 to 247. He tries a third time, and the proportion is 739 to 261. But when he comes to write up his results in a technical journal he does not state that the true proportion is 746 to 254 if the seeds are sown on a Wednesday, but 753 to 247 for Friday sowings, nor does he say that the results show a regrettable lack of uniformity and cast serious doubts on the correctness of Mendel's deductions. On the contrary, he says that his observations *confirm Mendel's Law,* and that if the experiments were conducted on an infinitely large scale the ratio of 3 to 1 would be achieved.

This is really very interesting, because it shows how dependent upon presuppositions the scientist is bound to be, even in such a simple experiment as crossing peas. In the first place he decides quite arbitrarily that the day of the week is irrelevant. Next, he asserts that further experiment would yield a result which would be nearer to the desired 3 to 1 ratio, and he does this solely on account of a blind and unreasoning reliance on the notion that larger numbers of chances are somehow superior to smaller ones. Finally he has a quite irrational faith in mathematics, and a passionate belief that neat small figures such as 3 to 1 are somehow *truer* than a larger one such as 746 to 254, or an untidy one such as may be obtained by reducing this to its decimal ratio of 2.9370078740157480314960629921259842519685o3 to 1.

I am not suggesting that the geneticist is wrong, or that Mendel's Law is incorrect, but merely that even such a simple formula as this is not only loaded with presuppositions of a most extraordinary kind, but involves something which amounts to a reverence for mathematical relationships—which are, after all, nothing but figments (though very useful ones) of the imagination. I do not happen to be a Roman Catholic, and personally I am by no means inclined to believe in the wonder-working properties of the bones of saints as such, but such a belief seems to me to be quite as reasonable as the worship of whole numbers in preference to recurring decimals, or a reliance on statistical means. The tenets of even the strangest religious sects are surely no more bizarre than a belief that mathematical neatness is a quality of truth.

Over and above his respect for mathematics the scientist has a faith of a more fundamental kind, which is reflected in the fact that he would never consider that an experiment begun on a Wednesday would yield entirely different results from one undertaken on a Friday. He believes in the orderliness of the universe. He stakes his shirt on his faith that everything happens in such a reasonable and well-ordered fashion that the same experiment will give the same result, whoever makes the observations, and wherever or whenever they are carried out. Hydrochloric acid poured on limestone chips will generate carbon dioxide in any school laboratory the whole world round. The dwarf strain of pea will be recessive to the tall in a Bermondsey allotment as well as in the monastery garden at Brno. Water at 4° centigrade will be heavier than an equal volume of water at 1° or 7°, day and night alike, from St. Louis to Samarkand.

This characteristic sameness of nature is so commonplace that few people realise its importance, and yet if the contents of our universe did not behave in so regular and predictable a fashion no real scientific research would be possible. Observations would only have momentary validity, and the sole truth which science could yield would be that nothing could be forecast, no rules or hypotheses framed, no measurements undertaken. But granted that the system of nature is orderly, then it can be investigated and conclusions can be drawn, without the suspicion that nature itself may be playing tricks upon the observer either from malice or from inherent unreliability.

But although the scientist has always to assume that this orderliness is there, and will always be there, he does not actually *know* that nature will necessarily behave in such an obliging fashion. He certainly knows that in his own experience it does so, and that others have always found it a reasonable assumption to make. Neither mathematics, nor the reliability and orderliness of nature, have let others down in the past, and so he is confident that he can put his trust in them. Nevertheless, to do so is nothing but an act of faith of a type very similar to that demanded of Christians.

The scientist puts his trust in nature not being malicious, but having such constant properties in its relations with him that he can examine it and draw up hypotheses. The Christian does precisely the same. He assumes a goodness and orderliness in the relationship of God with man. He looks back into the past, and from the records of scores of thousands of men and women, great and small, famous or obscure, he finds that faith in particular attributes of God's nature, or in the efficacy of certain methods of conducting a relationship with him, has not in their experience let them down. This is good enough for him, and he adopts (by an act of faith or trust) the same concepts as those of his forebears. After 40 generations have asserted from experience that prayer is effective in human need and helplessness it would indeed be strange if he were to assert the opposite, and quite ludicrous to do so without either examining the evidence or putting the matter to very thorough test. It is not uncommon, however, for a young man or woman to say to their priest or minister, or to a member of a church, " I don't hold with prayer. I don't see that it could possibly work." But this is nothing more than a disguised way of saying " I know nothing at all about the matter, and whatever people may have found out during the last few thousand years amounts to nothing compared with my own opinion." And, oddly enough, the same person would be most unlikely to risk a similar statement in the field of science. We can hardly imagine them being fool-hardy enough to declare, even to their closest friends, " Physics is all nonsense. There is no such thing as elec-tricity, and as for the focusing of light by a lens—well, it just can't happen, that's all."

I have suggested that the experience of 40 generations has been that prayer (to mention only one incidental of the Christian faith) does not let them down. This may seem an extravagant statement, because of course there have been innumerable cases of people believing that their God has indeed deserted them, and we all know of occasions when congregations have prayed for rain and the drought has continued unabated, or of " national days of prayer " for goodwill among men which have been followed almost immediately by the outbreak of a war. Yet the situation in science is precisely the same, and once again the example can come from genetics.

From what is generally known of the mechanism of inheritance it would seem certain that if an organism is carrying a particular outfit of genes, its structure and appearance can be forecast. A child of two blue-eyed parents will be blue-eyed; the kittens of a black tom and a pure ginger she-cat will be ginger if male and tortoiseshell if female. The laws of heredity work as expected. But it happened some years ago that an agricultural geneticist who was working on the genetics of the evening primrose, discovered that in some plants a gene definitely known to be present did not show its effects in the flowers. It might have been quite reasonable to suspect that the laws of genetics were at fault, for they certainly appeared to have let him down in this instance, but he made the interesting discovery that there was a " position effect," and that one gene was unable to influence the plant if it were situated close to another particular and quite different gene carried on the same chromosome. He was able to prove this by breeding the same genes into specimens in which the chromosome concerned was broken and part of its material attached to another, so that the usual linear arrangement of the genes was altered.

So the failure of a genetic law to operate as expected turned out merely to be the result of an over-simplification. The law worked so long as certain other conditions were fulfilled, but not otherwise. And the situation in, for example, an apparent failure of prayer on some special occasion or in the private life of an individual, is very similar. Here, too, it is probably the understanding of prayer itself that is at fault; and in the absence of certain other conditions (sincerity perhaps, or repentance, or humility—terms as obscure and complex as the position effect of chromosomes) the expectations based on general experience are not fulfilled.

There are, however, certain things which are utterly reliable, and which never have even the temporary appearance of letting down the person who trusts in them. In science, mathematics seems to be in this category. Though really a matter of blind trust, our faith in mathematics is not misplaced. Two plus two always equals four, and the squares of a series of consecutive numbers are invariably found to be alternately divisible and indivisible by four. In precisely the same way, certain fundamental propositions of religious doctrine are found to be utterly reliable under all circumstances. " It is better to suffer injustice than to do injustice to others," and " It is better to give than to receive," are only two of the statements in this category.

" It is better . . ."—but surely the very word " better " implies some system of valuation which has its roots in the human mind, one might think. And this is perfectly true. Justice, injustice, multiplication, squares and square roots, odd numbers and even, are all concepts which man has introduced to describe certain relationships. But that does not mean that the relationships do not exist, or that the statements are unreliable. On the contrary, people have staked their shirts on some and their lives on others, and not once in human history have they been found to be wrong.

III

HYPOTHESIS AND DOCTRINE

Although the parallel between scientific and religious certainty is a close one there are certain differences in approach which are important. It is perhaps reasonable to say that theology, and the arts, and science too, are all concerned with somewhat different aspects of the same reality. The arts may be striving to interpret man's own experience of reality, whereas religion is concerned with its meaning and purpose, and science with its mechanisms. This is sometimes expressed by saying that religion is concerned with "why," and science with "how," and the arts with "what"; and perhaps this is not far from correct.

The "how" aspect of science can be seen in any piece of research, whether it is concerned with trying to discover large fundamental principles or mechanisms of quite limited application. My own experience is drawn from genetics and embryology, and at one time I was engaged on an investigation of no great importance into the eye structure of certain strains of that best friend of geneticists, the fruit-fly *Drosophila melanogaster*. There were several genes which caused variations in the structure of the compound eyes of this creature, and the problem was to trace the way in which the various optical components were modified during their development. At first sight this might seem to have been an investigation into *why* a fly carrying the genes "rough" or "split" or "glued" had certain irregularities of the eye lenses, but in fact it was a study of *how* these changes were brought about. All one had to do was to examine the development of the eyes in detail and see where the normal processes went off the rails in each of the three mutant strains. It proved possible to show that there was irregular cell division at a certain stage, or failure of one component to grow at the same rate as another, and to conclude that the genes concerned produced their effects by acting during particular and limited periods of the development of the eye discs. "Rough" was found to act on the sixth and seventh days of larval life, by halting the growth of cells of one particular type. "Split" acted from day 4 to day 8, and "glued" from one day earlier; both interfered with cell division, but "glued" increased above normal the amount of a secretion for the cone cells, whilst "split" decreased it.

These observations, like those of any scientific investigation, merely recounted the immediate prior causes of the effects under consideration. I was not concerned, as a poet might have been, with the beauty of the eyes of the tiny creatures in the laboratory flasks which formed their lifelong homes, and if in fact I found them beautiful (as I did) it was not my business *as a scientist* to say so. If the paper in the *Proc. Zool. Soc.*, Series A, vol. iii, had begun with the words "Gazing into the mysterious depths of the exquisitely formed facets of *D. melanogaster* (strain Oregon R) I pondered . . ." the editors would indeed have been surprised. Neither did I discourse, as an artist might have done, on their form and colour, or see mirrored in the distorted facets of "glued" some elusive truth about flux and change, or perfection and imperfection in nature; nor after the fashion of a philosopher did I attempt to divine the *reason,* the "why" which lay behind the sheer existence of the abnormal eyes or even of the flies themselves. I was restricted to making scientific statements of causal relationships.

Now some people think that this limitation of science means that science itself is superficial, or even irrelevant— except in so far as its discoveries can be used in technology to provide us with artificial rubber tyres for motor-cars, or with new man-made fibres for ladies' dresses. Others go so far as to say that the scientific view of nature is a sheer perversion, in that it annihilates things as they are and substitutes a meaningless chain of causes and effects. But I cannot agree with these views, because although there may not be much to be learned from the roughness of the eyes of *Drosophila* mutants I believe that science can show us certain truths which cannot be discovered by other means. Robert Boyle, whom I have already mentioned, declared that there were two chief ways of learning about the attributes of God : namely, the study of his word in the Bible, and the study of his works in nature. (He did not rule out other means, such as revelation.) In other words, he regarded nature as " God's other Bible," and science as the means of translating it. And in this I think he was right. Science reveals to us truth of a special and restricted variety, but yet of a kind which is perhaps unattainable by any other means. If we accept as Christians affirm, that truth is of God, or that God is truth, then the work of the scientist must in essence be an increase in religious knowledge.

But the limitation of science not only to a search for immediate causes but to causes which can be measured or at least treated statistically, has its dangers, of which the best-selling researches carried out by Professor Alfred C. Kinsey, in the United States, on *Sexual Behaviour in the Human Female* are a particularly good example. Quite apart from the mental gymnastics of that part of his work which involved recording the mating behaviour of skunks and monkeys and comparing it with the intimate relationships of humans, Kinsey's investigation consisted in asking 7000 " human females " between the ages of 2 and 90 about their " sexual performance." I do not propose to speculate as to how far the Kinsey leg was being gently pulled by the human females who " remembered making specific responses to psychologic stimulation as early as the age of three," but only to examine the presuppositions and the conclusion at which he arrived.

Kinsey presumed that there were indeed such entities as " human females " and that a statistical correlation between what they told him about their " total sexual outlet " and the survival or break-up of their marriages (where they had any) indicated either a common cause for both effects, or that the one was the cause of the other. Now this may seem a sensible assumption, but it is not. Everybody knows that oysters are in season when there is an "r" in the month, but the arbitrary division of the year into twelve sections, and their provisions with names of classical origin, is neither the work of the oyster's sex glands nor the cause of the reproductive cycles found in the Whitstable beds. Phenomena which happen to run parallel may not necessarily be related at all.

A more far-reaching error can be seen in one of his conclusions. In the 7000-word synopsis, Kinsey expresses the view that "there seems to be no single factor which is more important for the maintenance of a marriage than . . ." Than what? Understanding? A happy home? Children? Fidelity? Or just love? Strange to relate, the vital factor turns out to be none of these things, but just "the determination, the will that that marriage shall be maintained." If one should wonder just what rôle such an old-fashioned concept as love may play, one can look in vain. The human females were not even asked about it, and the word did not figure once in the entire synopsis. Yet the vital importance within the home of the growth of a deep and indestructible love between husband and wife or parents and children has been known to millions of people throughout the world for centuries, without the aid of questionnaires or monkeys.

How then did Kinsey come to make his extraordinary judgment? Presumably because when looking for the most active cause of durable marriages he started with a list of possible ones and in due course found a mathematical correlation. But his list did not happen to include the one cause which most people would have known from their own experience and that of previous generations to be the really important factor.

We need not be surprised if a scientist occasionally makes mistakes. Science may indeed be a means of discovering truth—and in an earlier chapter I have urged that this is the proper way of regarding it—but that does not necessarily mean that an individual who happens to be a scientist may not sometimes be mistaken. A research physicist or biologist is no more superhuman than a writer or a businessman, and he is just as liable to human error. Because of the mere limitation of human faculty—or even occasionally through carelessness—he may make a faulty observation, or draw the wrong conclusions from evidence and experiment. And the same is the case with other experts. The theologian may make mistakes too. Indeed he is perhaps particularly liable to do so because of the exceedingly difficult subject of his studies. But if he frankly admits that he has been mistaken, he fares very differently from a scientist, for the reaction of the public to such an admission varies very greatly, not with the status of the expert so much as with the type of knowledge in which he is proficient.

Theologians in particular are regarded rather unfavourably if they change their views. A bishop who admits that he has come to modify in some way his attitude towards even such a matter of Church order as the remarriage of divorcees is likely to be regarded as a typical example of a man who does not know his own mind, or whose opinions are not very firmly grounded. But a biologist who says that he has come to the conclusion that characteristics acquired during the lifetime of an organism may after all be inherited, is thought of as a man whose increased study of a complex matter has led him to improve upon his earlier theories. In recent years Newtonian physics has largely been replaced by the concepts of Einstein, but it is never suggested that professors of physics who adopt the new and quite different outlook are insincere or uninformed. Instead (and quite rightly) they are regarded as endeavouring from their highly specialised knowledge to come nearer to the truth, as represented in the newer theory.

Indeed, scientific theory is looked upon as a soundly based approximation to genuine knowledge and certainty. And provided that we are alive to the occasional error of interpretation this is not an unreasonable view, for the great majority of scientific findings are virtually indisputable and are based on a large amount of research carried out with great care and accuracy, and checked where possible by abundant experiment. When a number of observations point in the same direction, then a " theory " can be drawn

up, such as the Kinetic Theory of Gases, or the Theory of
Evolution, each of which gives an account in somewhat
general terms but covering a wide range of phenomena.
And from such theories, or occasionally (as in Mendel's
case) as a result of direct observation, "Laws" can be
evolved which give a prediction of what will happen under
certain circumstances. Thus Charles's Law states that at
constant volume the pressure of a gas increases proportion-
ately to the temperature—a fact which can be verified by
experiment. Mendel's Laws forecast the proportions of
hereditary traits to be found in the offspring of certain
crosses. Gauss's Law of Error can be used to forecast the
distribution of shots on a target, the expectation of human
life, the range of intelligence among school children, or the
number of umbrellas left in London's Underground trains.

If experience shows such generalisations to be false, then
the laws are revised or replaced by others of greater accuracy
—as in the case of Einstein's physics replacing the earlier
theories of Newton, or the Copernican cosmology sup-
planting the Ptolemaic system; but in general a scientific
law can be assumed to cover a wide range of predictions
with accuracy, and to represent a very great amount of
human experience. In this respect it is entirely parallel to
Christian doctrine—a fact which is not generally realised.
On the contrary, it seems often to be assumed that the
doctrines of the Christian Church are more or less arbitrary
statements, thrown out by some committee of greybeards
in the Dark Ages for no better reason than the wish to
formulate a series of highly unlikely propositions with which
people had either to agree or take the consequences of
persecution and violence. Tenets which come from centuries long past are certainly not considered to have any
far-reaching validity for our own day, or to carry any
particular authority. Scientific "laws" on the other hand
are universally accepted as valid statements of fact, upon
which technological achievements can reliably be built.
And this notion of a difference in status between scientific
and religious teaching reflects the common belief that there

are several grades of experience and truth, some more respectable than others.

"Christ rose from the dead, did he? Well, you can't expect me to believe that without scientific proof." This is the immediate reaction of many a person to the central point of Christian doctrine, and one who takes this line will have no doubt at all that he is being perfectly reasonable. Yet he would not regard as rational a person who applied the same rule in reverse. "You say that the ocean tides are caused by resonance to the repeated pulls of the sun and the moon on water masses of suitable dimensions? My dear fellow, you can't expect me to believe such an unlikely thing in the absence of theological proof, or at least a hint from the Council of Trent."

A Christian doctrine is the precise counterpart of a scientific hypothesis. It is first formulated as a proposition and then subjected to the test of experience. Just as a scientific hypothesis has to stand up to the exacting demands of repeated check by innumerable experiments, so a Christian doctrine cannot remain an article of accepted belief if the experience of human life is against it. In this way it differs from an act of faith; it is not a leap in the dark towards a position of promised but unseen safety, but an expression of what people by the million have found to be valid and in no way contradicted by what they discover during the events of their own lives. Sometimes doctrine has proved inadequate and has needed revision; for example, not many Christians to-day would believe in a devil in the Miltonian sense of a god on the negative side of zero, because the theory of a loving God permitting the devil to lay booby-traps for people is not easily tenable. Besides, we now know much more about the causes of unpleasant events and evil actions which once were simply dismissed as the work of Satan.

But if doctrine has sometimes to be changed, then this is surely not a sign of weakness in the system of belief but rather an indication of clearer vision. The same applies in the field of science. The Phlogiston Theory was once regarded as an adequate explanation of combustion, but eventually it was surrounded by so many difficulties (such as the fact that phlogiston would have required to be endowed with a negative weight) that it had to be replaced by the notion of oxidation. Yet it would be foolish indeed to regard this change as a retrogressive step, or even as a sign of weakness in chemistry as such.

Though religious doctrine and scientific hypotheses are in much the same category, both can run over into dogma. A good example of this is in the case of the principles of the Conservation of Energy, and the Conservation of Matter—both of them now somewhat superseded by atomic physics, in which the distinction between energy and matter has largely disappeared. The conservation principle held good in chemical experiments in that the final energy of a closed system could be shown to be the same as the initial energy, but it was not long before scientists began to extend the principle to make declarations about aspects of reality concerning which, by the very nature of things, they had no knowledge at all. Matter came to be regarded as eternal and indestructible—the old cry of " They'll never split the atom " was derived from this belief—and the total energy of the universe in all eras of time and under all conditions was declared to be constant. Both these assertions were dogmatic; that is, they were extensions of hypotheses into realms where they could not possibly be checked by experience. Dogma, whether in science or religion, is dangerous; for when the formulation of ideas passes right out of the realms of human experience it can often mislead. Besides, it may be a contradiction of truth, the same truth of which the research scientist and the religious philosopher are each striving to apprehend their proper part.

THE COSMIC CREATION

Among the assorted elementary beliefs of any Christian is
the conviction that the universe (which includes the Earth)
and its habitants (which include himself) are the work of
the powerful activity of God as creator. This is not necessarily a Christian belief; it is shared by Jews, and is to a
certain extent present in almost every religion; but if he
does not have this first plank of belief no man can call
himself a Christian. Deliberate and purposeful creation
by God is not only a main strand of the Old and New
Testaments alike, but without it there is no room for belief
in a deity which can measure up to Christian concepts.
Besides, a Christian is bound to believe that there is unity
of some sort between Christ and "the Father," and he
cannot maintain this if he at the same time fails to accept
the father (or creator) as real.

To a child, the sheer beauty and wonder of the world
make the proposition of a creator self-evident, but certain
theories and findings of science have to be faced if a person
of maturer years is to be abreast of discoveries and yet
believe in a creation. Plenty of clichés are uttered on the
matter of creation—for instance, that the mere existence
of the world is strong evidence for a creator; or that it is
fruitless to talk of things having originated through randomness, because this only means that one has thought up the
new name of "randomness" to replace the older title of
God. But I doubt if the rather cheap points scored in such
ways are adequate to provide the picture of a creator which
a Christian must have; for his creator must be thought of
as wise, purposeful, thoroughly good, and loving.

Now the assertion of a Christian that the universe is the
handiwork of a God of this kind is quite dogmatic—and
so for that matter is the opinion of the atheist who declares
the reverse. They can neither of them have *direct personal*

experience of the beginnings of the universe in the past—
if indeed the universe ever had a beginning and is not right
outside the railway-timetable scheme of time with which
our thoughts are so preoccupied. One may learn about
God's love through personal experience, but not about
God as the prime source of all matter and energy and life.
This is no new problem. It has exercised the minds of
philosophers since time immemorial, and it is a very different matter from the mere acceptance or rejection of Genesis
I as an actual history of events—to which we shall have
to return in another chapter.

Creation is not to be thought of as confined to a beginning of the universe, or to the manufacture of some primeval form of life, or to the production of mankind. That
is, it *can* be regarded in such a way, but certainly not by the
Christian, for such a view is incompatible with his concept
of God. It may be much easier to conceive of a creator
who wound up the universe like a grandfather clock in
12,000,000,000 B.C. or thereabouts, and left it to tick on its
own; but this is not enough. The Christian believes in
a God who is active, and not in one who exhausted himself
in one great creative effort, nor in one who occasionally
rises from his couch to perform something new once every
few million years when the time seems to be ripe—or
perhaps merely because prolonged inactivity is becoming
somewhat boring. He believes in a God who not only
began but sustains even at this moment the entire universe.

The difficulties raised by science are of two kinds : those
concerned with the method of creation, and those which
merely imply that the purposeful creation of the Earth and
mankind is unlikely. Taking this latter group first, we
can note that science as a means of knowing immediate
causes neither denies nor confirms religious assertions (or
atheistic ones either); but by increasing our knowledge
of the sheer scale of time and space it gives us a very different picture from that which earlier generations had in front
of them.

Firstly, there is the sheer vastness of the universe. Our
Earth is certainly a handsome mass of rocky materials, but

its size in relation to the rest of the universe is ludicrously small. It trundles along through space, swinging round the giant Sun in an orbit more than 90 million miles in radius, spinning as it goes. It is only one of a family of several planets, and our Sun itself is in turn only one among thousands of millions of stars roughly spread out in the galaxy which we ingenuously call the " Milky Way." Within this huge arena the stars themselves are distributed so thinly in relation to the available space that our Sun's nearest neighbour is so far removed from our own little cosmic parish that even an object travelling with the vast velocity of a sputnik would take 150 thousand years to pass from the Earth to the nearest star. Light travels (in our worldly experience at least) at the fantastic speed of more than 180 thousand miles in a single second, and at this pace even the light we receive from the Sun takes more than eight minutes to cover the distance from the Sun to the Earth. Yet the light from the nearest of the other stars would require more than four years to reach us, and there are members of the Milky Way so distant that their faint light which to-night makes them appear visible to us has been engaged for the past 50 thousand years in traversing the intervening space—and that at a speed which would take an aircraft from London to Tokyo in a twelfth of a second.

But the Milky Way, itself a conglomeration of stars and nothingness so colossal that our solid Earth seems to shrink into utter insignificance, is by no means the only such galaxy. Others are known and charted, not by the dozen but by the million, spread out over such inconceivable distances of space that the light which is focused by the lenses of our modern telescopes to record their faint portraits on photographic plates started on its journey towards us millions of years ago—and in some cases long before the first amphibian creatures of our own world slowly crawled out of the brackish water of the Devonian seas, 3 million centuries before the Christian era !

Is it really conceivable that in the midst of all this vastness God could have bothered with a locality of such infinitesimal size as the Earth, or could have been concerned with the structure of its creatures, with the development of man, and with local events occurring during the governor-ship of Pontius Pilate at the eastern end of a patch of water which we call the Mediterranean, but the mere existence of which is as transient in the geological history of the Earth as a flicker in the flame of a candle? A person who knows anything at all of the vastness of the visible universe as revealed by modern astronomy may well be pardoned if he wonders whether there is any purpose or meaning in the existence of the Earth on which he lives. There is no scientific reason to think that the rest of the universe would in any way be affected if the world and all its inhabitants were to disappear and perish overnight—or that the creator (if there is one) would even notice the event.

But if to-day mankind sometimes feels lost in the inter-stellar void, then this is nothing new, and all the discoveries of astronomy have done no more than underline the senti-ment expressed by the writer of Psalm 8. " When I consider thy heavens, the work of thy fingers, the moon and the stars, which thou hast ordained; What is man, that thou art mindful of him? and the son of man, that thou visitest him?" These lines might have been written in our own day—apart perhaps from their insistence on the fact that the stars *are* the work of God's fingers and that he *is* in close personal contact with mankind.

No, the vastness of the universe is no sudden fresh discovery; and if we ourselves feel lost in the maze it is only because of the relative proportions of earthly and unearthly dimensions. Yet this is curiously irrational, for there is no inherent reason why size and importance should be thought of as proportional. The massive cliffs of Dover are built of the bodies of microscopic organisms. A single virus, too small to be visible by even the highest optical magnification which a microscope can achieve, can proli-ferate and set up reactions which can kill an all-in wrestler. A single molecule of an enzyme can be vital to the con-tinuance of the life of a creature weighing half a ton, and a microscopic pollen grain can give rise to a giant

Douglas fir of the forests of British Columbia. It is true that all these examples involve *life*—but so does the creation. In any event, it is obvious that the mere matter of dimensions is not necessarily an indication of power or importance.

But besides this, the feeling that God, if he exists, could not be concerned with the Earth suggests on the one hand that God is as limited in ability or thoughtfulness or consideration as a man may be—and this is hardly a Christian doctrine. It also implies that the Earth is the only thing in the universe which matters at all, and that all the rest is either useless or a mere display of creative virtuosity. Inevitably, we have no actual knowledge of the events which may be taking place elsewhere in the universe; and even on the Moon, which is a mere ¼ million miles distant from us, if there were cows (which there almost certainly are not) a moon-calf would need to be the size of St. Paul's Cathedral to be visible through our telescopes as a moving speck. But there is no reason whatsoever, other than sheer conceit, to imagine that a creator is so preoccupied with man and his Earth that the rest of the universe is so much scrap metal and rubble and incandescent gas. For all we know, sentient beings very like ourselves, or others much wiser, or creatures less capable of abstract thought and spiritual searching, may be dotted about throughout the length and breadth of the Milky Way, and some of them may feel as perplexed and lost as many of ourselves.

The human mind is much given to speculation. Some years ago, at the time when there was a press rumour that a flying saucer full of scaly little men had landed on our planet, I was talking to a friend who was a cathedral dean. "Do you realise that at any moment such a vehicle might land right here in Deanery Yard?" he said. "And if so, that it would be my job as an ordained priest and minister of the gospel to go out there and talk to the crew about the risen Christ? I confess that I find myself singularly ill-equipped for the task." I could not help the dean to be more prepared though perhaps that did not greatly matter, for the Deanery is still undisturbed and there are as yet no flying saucers parked on the cobbles outside; but at least it occurred to me that the little scaly men might have considered it their own pressing duty to preach to him about some revelation which had been theirs, and even that they too might have had the Incarnation on their own planet—and that they had perhaps not been so typically human as to crucify Christ. In our own day Christ would not be crucified either. He would be given his expenses to appear in a radio or television interview, then politely laughed at, and forgotten.

These speculations, like all such thoughts, are intriguing but fruitless. We can only reason about that which we know, and if we return to consider our place in the creation we have to admit that we are obsessed with the notion of size, that we judge the creator's ability and interest by our own simple standards of action, and that we have an unwarranted idea that nothing can really be as important as ourselves. And if we try to put these things aside we realise that the mere size of the universe is really quite irrelevant to the question of a creator.

Very similar doubts and wonderings are bound up with the time scale of the universe. And here the problem is newer, and one of which the author of Psalm 8 was quite unaware. We know (and I hope that fundamentalists will accept that this really is the case) that the world itself is at least 3,500,000,000 million years old; or rather, that if this is not the case then there are only two other explanations of the evidence yielded by measurements on the radioactive content of the rocks of our Earth. The first alternative is that all knowledge is illusion—a comforting escape route when applied to facts which emotionally one may want to reject, but not quite so satisfactory when one is falling in love, and still less so if one takes a motoring holiday in France, and decides that there is no objective reason for accepting the general experience that the right-hand side of the road is the one on which the local inhabitants happen to drive. In any event, whether comforting or not, the question whether knowledge is illusion is hardly a profitable matter for discussion.

The second possibility is that the long past of the Earth,

and the vast geological time scale of the prehuman ages is bogus, and was deliberately designed by God to mislead professors (and others too) very much in the way that the Piltdown remains were ingeniously planted as a highly successful private joke. A few people really believe this to be the case, and appear to think that God created the whole world in more or less its present state only a few thousand years ago, supplying it with uranium ores and fossils and water-worn rocks and the apparent remains of long-extinct volcanoes, all of which give an impression of age. But quite apart from wondering why such an extraordinary deception should be necessary, this view of the creator puts him squarely in the class of forgers, along with the man who drills worm-holes with a dental drill in sham antique furniture, or the clever artist van Meegeren who painted Vermeers. It is hard to see how such a swindler could be regarded as a God of truth. Besides, a God who has tried to fool mankind about the world which he has to inhabit might not necessarily be beyond tricking him again over the Incarnation; so the fundamentalist view is not so comforting as it might appear.

The feeling that time and relative value are proportional goes even deeper than the notion of the importance of size. Any individual who wants to impress others with the vital nature of his daily work can be relied upon to tell them that he rarely leaves the office until seven in the evening, that he brings home papers which occupy his whole attention till midnight or after. He is most unlikely to smile at his acquaintances and answer them somewhat in this fashion : " My work ? Oh, of course it's very confidential, but it doesn't take much of my time. I usually get through it in an hour or so and then put up my feet on the desk or go off for a round of golf." This, no doubt may be just how some executives occupy their day, but they would never say so. It would at once be assumed that their occupation was a trivial one and that they themselves were men of no consequence.

The Earth, according to a wealth of very reliable evidence, has existed for several thousands of millions of years. Yet the total human occupation of our planet dates back to less than a million years ago, and the Christian era cannot be thought of as even a drop in the bucket of geological time. Numerous comparisons have been put forward to illustrate this—for example, that if a diary of the history of the earth had been kept, and only one page allocated to describing the events of every thousand years, then the volumes of the diary would occupy two whole miles of library shelf but the record of human civilizations would be encompassed in only the last seven or eight pages, and the history of the Christian era would figure only on the two sides of a single leaf. But such a parallel, if taken seriously, is wholly misleading, for it is based on the assumption that the relative importance of events can be measured by the space allotted to them—a theory which can be dismissed by a glance at any Sunday newspaper.

" A thousand ages in Thy sight are like an evening gone," wrote Isaac Watts in one of his most famous hymns. This is true enough, but at the same time we must remember that we chalk up the ages in a quite arbitrary way as though we are compiling a railway schedule, working on the assumption that a thousand years (or a thousand revolutions of the Earth round the Sun) of the Ordovician period are equal to a thousand years in our own historic age. Yet there is not the slightest reason to suppose that this is a real equality; it is one imposed by ourselves with our factory time-clock outlook. Even if it were convenient for us (which it often is not) to measure the past in units of linear time scale, there is no validity in the system beyond the fact that we happen to use it. The life of St. Paul, we say, was a mere 70 years—against a total of 70 million for the Cenozoic period; but to regard 70 million years as a period a million times as great as 70 years is, strange though it may seem, an unwarrantable conclusion —indeed a survey of the main events which have taken place in the history of the world makes it seem a very unwise one.

Why do we use a linear and decimal arithmetic system for measuring time, instead of some other? We might equally well use the notation of the electronic calculator which knows only two numbers (0 and 1) but gets there just the same; or we could perhaps employ a system of square roots, or cube roots, or even a logarithmic scale. Sometimes I have a suspicion that the last of these might be a more suitable one, and at least it has the virtue of running in reasonable proportion to the *events* which have taken place on the Earth.

It is not altogether impossible to draw up a list of these major happenings, and for a scientifically informed Christian they would include such diverse items as the appearance of life on the Earth, the giving of " Old Covenant," and the Reformation. A brief list, scored in years and what we can call " log^{10} age," is given below—and the very fact that we have no word for a logarithmic measure of time is a reflection on the ease with which we assume certain mathematical habits of thought in preference to others.

It can at once be seen that these figures of log^{10} age give a reasonably regular series such as would form a comparatively straight line on a graph. Human history now occupies more than a third of the total span, and the period from

Event	Years ago	Log^{10} age (to 1 decimal place)
Origin of the Earth	3,500,000,000	9.5
First organisms	1,000,000,000	9.0
Life on land	300,000,000	8.5
First mammals	170,000,000	8.2
Anthropoids	30,000,000	7.5
Beginnings of Pliocene era	12,000,000	7.1
Dryopithecus radiates	4,000,000	6.6
Ape-men	1,000,000	6.0
Swanscombe man	400,000	5.6
Neanderthalers	100,000	5.0
Homo sapiens	50,000	4.7
Civilisations begin	8,000	3.9
Old Covenant	3,830	3.6
New Covenant	1,930	3.3
European expansion of the Church	1,200	3.1
Reformation	440	2.6
Expansion into mission fields	150	2.2
Ecumenical movement	30	1.5

Luther to our own day is quantitatively twice as great as the period of more than 3000 million years from the beginnings of the Earth down to the emergence of the mammals.

There are of course several objections. For example, there is no reason why I should have selected log to the base of 10, except that this happens to be the only set of tables I have in the house. Nor is there any valid reason for working backwards from the current date; nor even for counting in terms of " years ago " at all. And the whole hypothesis is an example of the dangerous and insidious temptation which can lead scientists to be carried away into the activity of " back-casting "—that is, the formulation of a scheme and the selection of data to bolster it up. In this instance there is no reason for choosing Swanscombe man and the Neanderthaler as landmarks and omitting the vitally important time of the beginnings of science in the seventeenth century, except that the Swanscombe and Neanderthal dates fill an otherwise awkward gap and the Scientific Revolution would obtrude a somewhat unwelcome figure into the series! Yet even if the table is not taken seriously it at least illustrates that an unusual system of time measurement may give tidier and less frightening results than that which we habitually use. The real point, however, is that *both* systems are quite arbitrary inventions of our own, and there is no reason to believe that the time scale of the creation is more truly measured in the one than in the other.

Quite apart from this, we have no warrant either as Christians or atheists, clock-makers or teachers, to believe that railway-timetable time has any validity outside our own Earth. It may well be as meaningless in the remainder of the Milky Way as a political splinter-group's programme for the reform of the school examination system would prove in the context of the moon—where there are neither school exams to be taken, nor votes to be solicited from an electorate.

Sooner or later, any person who pauses to consider things at all is brought up against the need to formulate some belief or other about the existence of the universe and its contents. He may believe that the universe " arose " for no reason or purpose, or that it is the work of a powerful and loving creator; he might even consider that the whole affair was created by the spirit of practical joking in order that men might waste time in speculating about it. But the prime cause is beyond demonstration, and must remain so. All that a man can do is to choose his theory and endeavour to test it so far as he is able by his own experience and that of others. The Christian makes certain assumptions, based on tradition, the assertions of the Bible, and perhaps on his own individual revelation; but neither he nor a non-Christian can derive from scientific measurement and description of the visible universe any confirmation amounting to proof of his belief. In either case he is thrown back upon trust, and upon pious (or impious) hope.

It is as well that this should be realised. In his attitude to the creation the Christian is largely dependent upon a prime cause which he apprehends from other data and by other means. He believes in God, but not because of astrophysics. Similarly, an astrophysicist is concerned with measurement, and with trying to discover immediate physical causes. Probably he himself knows only too well the limitations of his science, but his public may not always realise that if he says that he finds no evidence for a creator he is in fact saying what he should do. " No man hath seen God at any time "—and certainly not on the plate of the Schmidt reflecting telescope.

Many scientists have declared, however, that their studies of the universe have brought them face to face with the divine. Einstein himself wrote of his " humble admiration of the illimitably superior spirit who reveals himself in the slight details we are able to perceive with our frail and feeble minds," and he stated that this was his idea of God. Yet in saying this he was not speaking as a scientist, but as Albert Einstein, and he was merely expressing in modern language the same conviction as that of the author of Psalm 19—" The heavens declare the glory of God." The heavens can declare this glory to scientists and to non-scientists alike.

Science may show space to be vaster and the galaxies and stars more complex and more orderly than we might once have supposed, but in itself it can provide no actual warrant either for belief or for disbelief. Astronomy can intrigue or terrify, or it may enthral; but it cannot attempt to answer the ultimate problem of why the universe is there at all.

But if astronomy cannot answer the age-old wonderings of man, it can at least have implications. Clearly it had for Einstein, and even the non-expert may feel that the wonders unfolded by modern research lend to the universe an awe and beauty, a majesty of power and orderliness which could not have been revealed by any other means. To a religious person with no doubts about the creation, each new enlargement of our knowledge only makes the universe the more magnificent, and God the more astoundingly gracious in his contact with man. On the other hand, a person of little or no faith is more likely to have his doubts and scepticism increased.

This is particularly the case in the matter of the actual formation of the planet on which we sweep through space at some 60,000 miles per hour. Our distant forefathers were able to think of the Earth itself as having been specially created for their benefit and as the stage on which the great drama of man's obedience and disobedience could be enacted. To-day there are several theories as to the actual mechanics of the origin of our world, and though they can never be more than speculative they are reasonable enough. Our planet may have been formed along with the others when two stars (of which our Sun was one) passed close enough to each other for their mutual attractions to tear out some of the materials and leave it as swirling eddies which cooled, slowly solidified, and took up the courses of the planetary orbits; or perhaps a supernova explosion, the disintegration with incredible violence of some distant and unknown star, hurled into space the mass of material which now forms our Earth, sending it flying through space until by good fortune it became trapped in the Sun's gravitational field and its path was bent into a suitable ellipse; or our planet may have begun as a condensation in the solar nebula, increasing in size as meteorites collided with it in headlong flight. There is no need for us to examine the evidence—there are schools of thought supporting each of these possibilities. But all the theories have one thing in common, namely that the birth of the Earth was the result of nothing but accident.

Faced with this, the Christian may wonder how he is to integrate an apparent cosmic accident with his notion of a planned and purposeful creation. Is he to think that an omniscient and precognisant God so framed the universe that such an event was a foregone conclusion? Or is he to believe that the apparent accident was " arranged " and staged, God himself knowing that the conditions which would eventually appear on the Earth would be just right for the development of mankind? Or is he to take refuge in the probabilities and improbabilities of mathematics and comfort himself with the feeling that sooner or later, throughout the length and breadth of the universe, such a fortunate catastrophe was bound to occur; and that God, as it were, waited for it to happen? And if so, what do we mean by God " sustaining " the whole creation even at this moment?

I doubt if a Christian need lose much sleep over these problems. To attempt to fit God into a mathematical concept of gravitation or statistical chances is to try to bind him to the scale and time of worldly events alone, and to suggest that God can somehow be found in the universe rather than *the universe itself in God*. The Christian—and indeed any inhabitant of the world—is obliged to take the Earth as existing, and he may also realise that not all things are accessible to his knowledge. He may be able to describe in terms of measurement the little patch of universe in which he lives, yet such faith as he has does not depend upon the method of planetary formation, nor upon the constituents of interstellar space, but stems from experiences of a very different order.

V

LIFE AND SERVO-SYSTEMS

Science gives us an awe-inspiring and intriguing picture of the extent of the universe, and it provides an account of the possible mechanics of the origin of our planet in the interstellar void. Its theories and discoveries about the nature of the universe may well cause the Christian (and the agnostic too) to wonder, but they do not in any way supplant or destroy the religious belief in a purposeful creator—any more than an analysis of the " Eroica " symphony in terms of harmony and counterpoint can exorcise the spirit of Beethoven. No, the scientific view is not an alternative choice in the sense that we must choose between a supernova explosion and a creator; it merely gives us a special insight into a realm of reality where many truths and matters of detail would be undiscoverable by other means.

Yet the fundamental difference between the picture provided by scientific research and the teachings of religion is even more sharp when we come to consider the age-old question, " What is man?" Mankind as a species is as susceptible to scientific investigation as anything else, but the theories of science inevitably strike nearer home—so very close that they are always with us, even in our most intimate relationships of home and family.

The Christian view of man is most easily summed up in a phrase borrowed from the pre-Christian writings of the Old Testament : man is created *in the image of God*. This does not mean that the Christian should regard God as a kind of enlarged specimen of *Homo sapiens* situated somewhere outside the world, but rather that God has conferred upon man some of his own qualities. It is not a matter of shape and structure, but of attributes. Love, and the seeking for freedom, for justice and right, the joy

46

of creating things of ingenuity and beauty, and the ability to forgive—these are just a few of the human qualities which to the Christian are not purely haphazard but are aspects of the divine which are mirrored in the nature of the individual. That is not to say that all men are loving or easily loved, nor that forgiveness or the desire to create things of beauty are characteristics which mark the whole life of every human being. Clearly this is not the case. But when the Christian talks of man as being created in the image of God he means that God has certain abiding qualities which are faintly mirrored in man himself. How clearly they are mirrored is another matter, for one of the qualities is freedom to choose—and the choices deliberately made by each of us are sometimes foolish, and frequently deliberately wrong.

In this short statement of the Christian concept of man I have had to use a number of terms which involve certain presuppositions—for instance, that there is such a thing as right; and that free will actually exists. The first of these is not a matter on which science as such has any opinion, and if sometimes individual scientists have tried to introduce other systems of judgment to replace the yardstick of right and wrong they have merely been acting as men, and not as scientists. They might equally well have been golf-course designers or trapeze-artistes. But upon the matter of free will the discoveries of research have, as we shall see later, a very considerable impact.

The reader may be surprised that in this outline of the Christian notion of the nature of man I have said nothing about an actual relationship between God and the individual, nor mentioned such things as the ability to be redeemed. But there is a reason for this omission. It is perfectly true that a Christian would regard some awareness of God to be the real hall-mark of humanity, but the very intimate relationship which means so much to the individual Christian is not a characteristic of *man* but a demonstration of the grace and generosity of the God who can be bothered with mankind at all. One has only to read the daily newspaper to be astounded that God can be so patient as to deal with man at all instead of leaving him to stew in the very unpleasant juice he so continually makes for himself. That this relationship of love and grace and forgiveness exists is something about which the Christian cannot have any doubt at all, but it is not a result of the nature of man. It depends entirely upon the nature of God.

The scientific concept of man is very different, and extemely complex. An anthropologist may describe man as a tool-using animal, but the scientific study of mankind involves very much more than a digging up of the pre-historic past. It may be concerned on the one hand with a study of protein structure and chain molecules, and on the other with palaeontology and climatic variations or the electrical organisation of nerve paths and conductor systems. But fundamental to all such studies is the matter of life itself. The Christian regards the sheer existence of life as perhaps the chief among the reflected attributes of a creative God and he thinks of man as being in a very special category; yet the scientific concept of life is rather different.

At first sight the difference between living and non-living things seems obvious enough. A collection of samples of metal ores in a museum case remains where it is, immobile, constant in form and in number. Live things on the other hand behave quite differently. Inanimate objects are immobile except in so far as they are moved about by wind and wave and earthquake, or by living things, but live objects may be able to move under their own power. This attribute applies only to animals (as opposed to plants) and not necessarily to all animals either—for example, many sea-anemones, and the crinoids, and vast numbers of parasites remain rooted throughout life to the spot on which they first happened to alight. Nevertheless, movement is a general characteristic of animals at least.

Even more striking and universal is the fact that a living organism does not remain constant in form. On the contrary, it grows. Nor does an assemblage of live creatures remain constant in number. Organisms reproduce themselves—and they die, too. From the scientific point of view

the death of an organism (and of a person) is in no way
different from the eventual failure of a machine. Driven
continually, an automobile will periodically need servicing
by a garage mechanic, but sooner or later the walls of the
cylinders are worn down, the bearings begin to disintegrate,
the insulation of the coil or magneto may develop faults,
the ignition condenser loses its dielectric capacity, the teeth
of the gears and differential are worn, and the whole
machine becomes grossly inefficient. Repairs help to stave
off the final day, but eventually some vital part is damaged
beyond repair, and the automobile no longer functions. The
petrol which it drinks and the air which it inhales through
its carburettor are still available, but the machine will no
longer work. It is consigned to the scrap heap.

To the biologist the death of an organism is very similar.
Running repairs are carried out by the production of new
tissue, but there comes a time when the creature is altogether too inefficient. The breakdown of some vital part
ensues, and though in the case of man the final dissolution
may be postponed for a little while by drugs and surgery
and therapy, the failure of the complex machinery of life
is sure to come. The creature dies, and that is the end
of it. The Christian accepts the reality of this outlook
except that he denies emphatically that physiological failure
is necessarily the end of things, so far as man at least is
concerned—a fundamental piece of his faith to which we
shall return later.

Even the simplest creature may appear to be organised
in much greater complexity than a machine, and to work in
ways which are fundamentally different. However, recent
speculation in biology forces one to wonder whether these
differences are really as clear-cut as they seem. If an
organism is viewed as a complex arrangement of servomechanisms some of the special characteristics of life at
once begin to disappear. A servo-mechanism is merely an
arrangement by means of which a small application of
energy can set in motion a mechanical response which is
out of all proportion to the stimulus. An example is in the
braking system of a modern bus, in which air is sucked

either by the intake of the engine or in some instances by a separate pump, so that a partial vacuum is formed in a stout cylinder. This vacuum is on one side of a piston, which is accordingly forced by the atmospheric pressure of 14 lb. per square inch towards that end of the cylinder. This air pressure works against powerful springs, the compression of which it is just sufficient to overcome. The piston itself is connected by rods to the brake-shoes, and so the pumping out of the air from the cylinder has the effect of holding the brake-shoes clear of the surface of the brake-drums on the axles. The braking pedal is connected to a valve, and when it is pressed it does no more than admit air into the partial vacuum, but the result is that the suction is broken, the piston flies back under the action of the strong springs, and the brake-shoes are clamped against the wheels. By this means quite a gentle pressure exerted by the driver's foot has the result of releasing a very considerable force, which is distributed over the lining of the brake-drums.

Another example of a servo-mechanism is seen in the automatic garage door. The door is raised by an electric motor, which is set in motion by a magnetic or mercury tip-switch, which in turn depends for its operation on an electric current derived from an amplifier. The input to the amplifier is no more than a very faint current derived from a suitably sheltered light-sensitive selenium cell on the frame of the door, and when the owner of the garage drives in at his gate and the beam from the headlamp of his car strikes the cell, a current is set up which is amplified to operate the switch and cause the garage door to swing up ahead of the car. The arrangement is such that the very small stimulus of the headlamp beam triggers or releases an amount of movement which is out of all proportion to the energy supplied *in the stimulus*—though of course the energy has to come from somewhere and in this instance from the power station by way of the electric mains' supply.

Living creatures are very dependent on somewhat analogous mechanisms. Pavlov's famous dogs were trained so that the original smell-stimulus which caused the salivary glands to secrete quantities of fluid was replaced by the sound of a bell ringing—but in either case the mechanism was of the servo-type, in that a very small stimulus produced a considerable effect. A fly may sit on a cake, but the mere movement of a human hand so as to cause a shadow to shift across some of the tiny lenses of one of its compound eyes will result in the insect immediately taking flight. A lion may be standing motionless in the shadow of the African scrub when the appearance within its field of vision of the striped form of a zebra will send down its optic nerves a stimulus which is infinitesimally weak, but which will be relayed by the sympathetic nerves to contract the walls of the blood vessels, raise the blood pressure, and thus increase the supply of oxygenated blood to the muscles. The net result is that the small visual stimulus produces a high state of physiological activity, and the lion can spring with even more deadly effect than if the prey had not appeared.

Similarly, in the mating behaviour of many creatures a stimulus of no measurable strength can set off a complex train of responses which may involve a great output of energy. A few molecules of a complex aromatic chemical produced by a female moth may set off behaviour in the male which will send him flying a mile or more up wind. Coloured feathers of a male can trigger vastly complicated reflexes in a female. All through nature the pattern is much the same—an animal is so constructed that a large amount of energy or physiological activity can be triggered by very weak stimuli acting on specially designed receptors.

Now this is all very wonderful, and any naturalist may well be amazed at the intricacy of design which lies behind even the simplest piece of behaviour of an animal; but the question arises whether the creature itself is not just a vastly complex machine. If a fly takes flight because of a change in the intensity of illumination falling upon its light-sensitive ommatidia, in what way is it really different from the automatic garage door which opens when the beam of a headlamp falls upon its receptor? Servomechanisms, particularly when linked up by automation, are able to carry out processes almost indistinguishable from those which are characteristic of live creatures.

Automation is the automatic and self-regulating control of processes in manufacture, the various stages being controlled in many instances by " feed-back " of information as to the state of affairs a step farther down the line. It is not difficult to imagine a plant for the manufacture of beer bottles where sand, soda-ash, and limestone are fed from the stockyard to an automatic mixer which delivers the frit to a furnace, from the other end of which the molten glass emerges in dollops to fill the chambers of a rotating mould in which the bottles are blown. The furnace is heated by gas, and a thermo-couple accurately controls the viscosity of the glass by cutting down the gas supply when the temperature reaches a certain figure.

The gas and temperature control is of course a commonplace and simple form of feed-back, but the whole manufacture can be linked in its various stages. A crisis in the warehouse will lead to an immediate increase in stock, the feed-back from which will slow the delivery belt. This change can automatically cut down the rate of blowing and moulding. This in turn involves less molten material being taken from the furnace, and another feed-back mechanism will ensure that less sand and other ingredients are carried in. Less cold frit has now to be heated, and the gas supply is decreased—and so on.

The parallel between such an arrangement and the workings of an organism is obvious. We ourselves take in food to our mixer and digester (the stomach) whenever it is presented. Some of the product is used for oxidation to provide heat, and some is carried to the muscles for later use. Still more may be stored as fat—a reserve stockyard. We breathe air, and the heart maintains the circulation of oxygen and raw materials all round the body. Yet the balance is maintained by feed-back systems working with the most meticulous accuracy. If a stockbroker runs for a bus, his muscles use glycogen and more is at once delivered to the site. The working of the muscles demands more oxygen, and the heart speeds up. So does the rate of breathing, as we can more easily notice. At the same time the chemical transformations in the muscles generate heat, but the body's thermostat devices respond at once to the feed-back information, and the capillaries in the face dilate to give better radiation. A salty fluid is released over the skin as perspiration, the evaporation of which as the man later fans himself in the bus with his copy of the evening paper removes surplus heat in the form of latent heat of vaporisation, and though the man may "feel hot" his temperature is in fact kept all the while within a fraction of a degree of the normal.

If the parallel between automation and servo-systems on the one hand and the activities of living things on the other is so close, we can ask ourselves whether there is indeed any difference between an organism and a complex machine. And almost at once the answer will be forthcoming that the garage-door mechanism and the beer-bottle plant are each the creations of an engineer and could never have just "appeared" on building sites unaided; and so, by analogy, all creatures must similarly have a creator. Besides, the characteristics of life are not limited to controlled and balanced activity. Cannot even the humblest organism grow, and reproduce itself? Just how valid these objections may be we shall now have to consider.

VI

SELF-REPRODUCTIVE MACHINERY

It is certainly the case that growth and reproduction are absolute fundamentals of life, and in both these things an organism may at first sight appear to differ radically from a machine. An animal takes in grass, or the bodies of other animals, or bacon and eggs and chipped potatoes, and it takes in oxygen too. From these materials it produces the actual stuff of its own body, and adds to its weight and stature—quite apart from carrying out running repairs. It would indeed be handy if an automobile could do the same, so that one might buy the smallest family model, and allow it to mature during running until it became a six-seater limousine; but this does not happen. And if not, then is it not just because an organism has the special mysterious quality of life whereas the motor-car has not? There is no life without growth, and no growth without life—or so it would appear. Life and growth seem fundamentally and intimately linked.

Besides, mere growth is not all. Every living thing can actually make copies of itself. Whether it be a pine-tree manufacturing seeds at the base of the tough segments of its cones, or a wood-wasp darting its sharpened tube through half an inch of wood to lay its microscopic eggs inside some grub tunnelling within the stem, a whale giving birth to its young in the cold waters of the southern ocean, or a black aphis producing its young by the thousand on the leaves of some choice dahlia in the public park, every living thing can manufacture others in its own likeness. Automobiles, on the other hand, are made on a production line operated not by last year's models but by humans, and a pair of identical saloons kept in a garage will never give rise to a family of baby cars. This does not strike us as in the least remarkable. Reproduction is inseparable from that strange power or entity which we call "life." Living things can reproduce their own likeness, which no machine could ever do, one might confidently affirm. Yet the idea that a machine could never reproduce itself cannot be so easily held in these modern days of automation and servo-controls. It is in fact quite possible to conceive of an elaborate machine which could do just that very thing.

It is already commonplace for intricate and accurately fashioned components to be manufactured and machined without the constant supervision or control of an engineer. In the simplest instance a machine tool can be provided with a sample of a shaped piece of sheet metal (such as the door frame of a motor-car) and it will be equipped with a finger which runs round the outline and causes corresponding movements to be made by the bed of the machine so that an exact replica is sawn out from a sheet. The next stage is found in the more elaborate machine tool with alternative heads which come into operation in succession, each performing a different process. Simple objects such as screws may be made in this way, or much more complex items such as specially shaped and finished components for washing-machines. The machine tool itself is controlled by drawings, or by instructions recorded on magnetised tape, each process corresponding to a "tune" of signals on the tape. It carries out its work unaided, provided only that it receives materials on which to work, and power to operate the mechanism.

A still more advanced stage is seen where whole batteries of machine tools performing different functions are linked to each other by automation and feed-back, so that their individual products can be assembled (perhaps by other machine tools) into something more complex, and the rate of operation of each is governed by the intake of raw materials and the output of (for example) castings emerging from the furnace. In this way it is possible for all the components of a model of a car to be manufactured in the right quantities, all the processes being controlled by an electronic computer which receives information from the furnace conveyer belts. No personnel are needed other than a few white-coated electricians who act in a merely supervisory capacity—and who may all go to sleep without any disastrous results. There is a supply of raw materials from the stockyard hoppers, a supply of electricity from the mains, and that is all. The extremely complex manufacturing processes look after themselves.

Now this is not the same as an organism. A live creature produces copies of *itself* and not of nuts and bolts and windscreen-wipers. But let us suppose that an automative plant is built in which every process is neatly co-ordinated to cover each operation from raw materials to finished article. Its diggers and grabs keep up a supply of material to the furnace, which is heated by producer gas formed by passing air over heated coke made from the coal mined by the plant's own mechanical diggers. The molten metal is cast and machined by automatic tools, but in this instance the product is not an automobile but the very same outfit of conveyor belts, mechanical diggers, and machine tools with which the plant itself is equipped. Even the computer which organises and controls the whole affair is copied. In such a case the machine is *genuinely reproducing itself,* and its descendants will continue to do the same. Granted access to the necessary raw materials, the system can go on indefinitely—which is much the same situation as we find in organisms. Of course the machines will eventually wear out and break down or grind to a halt, but this does not matter in the least provided that there is time for each machine on the average to produce at least one of the next generation before it cracks up. This too is disconcertingly parallel to what we find in living organisms. Some die at birth, others in infancy, and all of them sooner or later; but on the average there is time enough to establish the new generation.

Clearly it is not unreasonable to think that engineers could design a machine which would carry on in this way, taking in raw materials, turning out a replica of itself, and eventually wearing out but leaving the younger one active. And if so, then it is not easy to see in what way such a structure would differ in essence from a living organism.

The special characteristics of living things—endowments, as a Christian would say, from the hand of the creator—have vanished.

Such a machine certainly needs the original work of a designer, but this " creator " need not have the qualities which a Christian states to be inherent in the God of creation. The engineer has to design the original model and see to its construction, but that is all. As soon as it is completed he can retire to Monte Carlo if he wishes, and not give his creation another thought. He does not have to keep it going, nor is he obliged to like it, let alone love it. He may even be glad to be rid of it. And in the case I have just outlined the creator (whom we can suppose to be the chief scientist and managing director of Pilkington Electronics, Ltd.) can die, and his firm may be wound up to pay the estate duty, whilst his creation goes ever onward, digging coal and ore, constructing duplicates of its machine tools, and setting one generation after another upon its mechanical way.

It is not altogether unreasonable of certain biologists or physicists if they look upon living things in this way. If one regards life as machinery, then there is no reason to believe from a study of life itself that there is an active creator in charge of maintenance and running. Mice in the cellar, yeast in the brewery vats, diphtheria bacilli on the jelly of the hospital culture plate, wire-worms in the lawn—is there really any reason to believe that they are sustained by an active creator, in whose absence their cell divisions and metabolism would suddenly cease?

To this, I think, the Christian can only say that the question is meaningless and represents a totally false view of the nature of life. It is not a matter of a creator sitting up above seven layers of cloud, drawing blue-prints for lapdogs and germs and humming-birds, and fitting out his models with dry batteries full of " life " energy. God is not turning out life as a mechanic, but life is in itself an attribute of God. The creation is not outside God, or under him; it is within him. The whole universe is, to the Christian, within God as much as his own duodenum is within himself. To speculate about what might or might not happen to his duodenum if he were elsewhere would be nonsensical. It is part of him, and he sustains it. It cannot exist without him, any more than life can exist without the surrounding and all-embracing God. We can note a further parallel too. Trouble in the duodenum —caused perhaps by a duodenal ulcer—can cause a man very acute pain. The Christian believes that trouble in the realm of living things causes acute pain to God. When processes go wrong and men do not use the astounding gift of life as they should, then there is a disease in the vast body of the universe which is within God. It may cause recurrent or perpetual pain, the agonising pain of crucifixion; but it does not kill God.

The difference which a Christian may see as dividing the self-reproducing machine which might be made by a technician and the existence of living creatures in the universe is simply this : the machine is apart from its maker; but life is a part of its creator. The reader may here suggest that this is not necessarily so, and that a mouse or a yeast cell, or a jelly-fish is indeed no more than a self-reproducing automative machine, whilst man is inherently different; but this is not the Christian doctrine of the creation. Christianity certainly recognises the distinctive nature of man, but it does not separate off the remainder of life as mere machinery. It is true that we often treat animals as machines, but that is our fault and not theirs. Christianity has never repudiated the view of the writer of Genesis I that God has created *all* forms of life and has charged man to " have dominion " over them as trustee.

Without the belief that the universe and all its contents are within God, then living creatures and self-perpetuating machines do not appear to me to be properly distinguishable. Mere ingenuity of design and the power of self-perpetuation are not evidence for a God adequate to measure up to Christian belief. And if the " simple " cell of a protozoan, or the segment of a tape-worm, is a mere packet of proteins and carbohydrates rather than an infinitesimal sample of the divinity of all things, then I cannot see why men should be differently regarded. True, a human can do many things that other creatures (so far as we know) cannot—for example, he can appreciate beauty, paint pictures, and play the piano—yet there is really no obvious reason why machines could not do the same. We already have computers which can play chess, with a chuckle if they win or a growl when losing; and to equip such a machine to spend some of its time splashing paint on canvas or hammering out on piano-keys a tune which conforms to certain relationships of harmony stored in its electronic memory would be no more difficult.

Of course there is more to man than mere competence in the arts. For instance, a Christian might say, man can praise his maker. Yet the mechanical engineer would immediately answer that his self-reproducing machines could without difficulty be equipped to do the same, and a tape-player could be incorporated so that every machine would repeat at intervals (and twice on Sundays) "Congratulations to the directors of Pilkington Electronics, Ltd. who designed me." And as a final touch a relay could be added so that just before complete breakdown and death a servo-mechanism would change the spool and the machine would solemnly utter the words "Pilkington Electronics know best. It was fun while it lasted, but this is the end." Or even "This looks like the end, but it isn't. My soul goes marching on—probably in the Pilkington Electronics board-room."

One might think that this was in no way comparable with the praise and prayers offered by Christians, who are not just equipped with tape recorders, yet we have to recognise that much of our emotions and responses are in the long run genetically determined, and the difference between the self-reproducing machine and a human is no longer quite so obvious as we could wish.

What I have said here may come as a shock to many, but instead of being horrified at the notion that technology might possibly achieve these wonders I hope the reader will seriously consider whether we should not be grateful to the electronics experts and servo-engineers for having thrown up the challenge to our thoughts. It is no longer adequate to think of the creation and of man in rather faint-hearted and feebly pious terms. If one thinks at all, it is necessary in this age of technical achievement to be quite certain of what one believes about life and the attributes of man.

To make a self-reproducing machine might be very clever, but it would be quite pointless; and the pointlessness is a very cogent matter, for if an organism were really no more than an automative system what would be the point of the existence of life at all, and of ourselves in particular? At worst, our whole existence would be nothing but accident, and at best no more than a vain show of ingenuity on the part of a creator—just as it would presumably be on the part of the directors of Pilkington Electronics, Ltd.—and man's adoration of his maker would really be no different from a built-in recital of praises emanating from a mighty Wurlitzer. But the Christian, conceiving of all life not as mere arrangement of mechanisms but as an inherent quality of God, has a very different view. The praise which he likes to sing on Sundays or offer in silence in the quiet of his own home is not played on a tape but is the reflection of the one thing above all others which distinguishes man from the animals—an awareness of God.

It is of course permissible to wonder whether this awareness is a mere deception. Freud suggested that religion is merely a system of providing an interpretation of things we cannot otherwise explain, and Marx described it as the " opium of the people " (a drug of wicked capitalist origin, no doubt). But I do not think we need take Freud very seriously. Just as Kinsey unfortunately forgot about love when investigating human females, so Freud could sometimes be blind to the obvious—as when he went to great lengths to explain the reason why a person who leaned out of an upper storey window stepped back for fear of falling out. (His explanation was in terms of a struggle against self-identification with an imaginary prostitute showing herself at the window to attract imaginary men walking down the opposite pavement. The possible explanation that a person might be afraid of falling out of the window because he was afraid of falling out of the window just did not occur to him.) Nor need Marx occupy much of our time. Opiates are very soothing to jaded nerves, but they are hardly adequate to lead a person into the life of energetic, courageous, and self-sacrificing devotion to others which has been the hall-mark of Christians by the million all down the ages.

Of course Freud and Marx would have been right if they had said that religion could sometimes be of the order they suggested. To some people religion (or Freudian psychology) is undoubtedly something of a refuge from intellectual bewilderment, and to others religion (or Marxism) can indeed have a drug-like effect in making them impervious to the needs or the fundamental human rights of others who happen to think differently. But that is beside the point, for the reality of an individual's awareness of God is as susceptible to proof as is anything else. The person who is aware will put it to the test, and it will not take him very long to discover whether or not he is apprehending a mere fiction. Awareness of God in some form or other is present in many religions, and in some it reaches a very high pitch, but the Christian asserts that he is aware of God in a unique and very personal relationship, and it is primarily on this personal experience, either in his own life or in that of others, that the Christian makes his choice as he does. He may start with doctrine or tradition, but sooner or later he will probably find himself in a position to test what he has heard, and when he discovers for himself the reality of God as his own sustainer he does not arrive at this conclusion by a detailed analysis of protein molecules and endocrine secretions. That man, composed of these complex organic arrangements, can indeed have the awareness at all is a never-failing source of wonder to him; but instead of trying to account for it in terms of electrical currents (or even psychoses) he thanks God for the gift of the awareness itself, which alone lifts him right out of the realm of machinery.

VII

THE MODE OF CREATION

Awareness of God, which the Christian believes to be the special attribute of man, involves very much more than a mere passive acceptance of the notion that a deity exists as a kind of super-stratospheric managing director. It includes some belief as to the character and quality of God. In the most primitive religions the chief attributes of a deity may be those of wrath and power, but to the Christian (and to the Jew) God is seen as being in some way the source of all ultimate goodness and right, whilst man has been deliberately created and given the responsibility and freedom to choose to co-operate in the achievement of God's purpose.

Even in this one aspect of Christian belief, the problems for a person living in the midst of great scientific discoveries are very considerable. How was man made, and what evidence is there of any purpose in his presence here on the Earth? Has man really any freedom of choice, or is he not rather the slave of inherited instincts and environmental conditions? Are goodness and right more than mere terms in which to dress up man's desires or current aims, in order to give them an aura of respectability?

None of these are questions which can be answered by the means of scientific proof, any more than the loveliness of a moonlit night or the beauty of a piano concerto by Beethoven can be demonstrated by similar means. Of course a Gallup poll or opinion sampling might prove that a great majority of people assert both these things to be delightful, but it can only discover *opinion* and not what is the true objective character of the things themselves. Just the same applies to the prime articles of Christian belief—they cannot be proved by scientific method. This is a fact which worries many people in an age when such proofs are very much *à la mode,* but it should not upset the Christian. His belief that these things are so rests on quite different grounds, and he can recall the stern rebuke which Christ himself gave nineteen centuries ago to those who imagined that everything would be satisfactory if only he would oblige by providing a sign or scientific proof of his authority.

This is not to say that a Christian can blindly accept anything. Divine purpose and freedom of will may not be demonstrable in terms of chemical experiments or the units of physics but at least the Christian cannot believe in them if all the evidence is flatly against them; and if he does not accept divine purpose and freedom of human choice then he cannot possibly be a Christian. He may still regard Christ as a rather able itinerant preacher and regret that he met such an early and unpleasant death, but that is something very different from the Christian faith.

The notion of a purposeful creation of man raised no problems in days when a Christian could simply accept the Bible as the word of God in the sense that it was from cover to cover an infallible source of detailed truth dictated by the deity to scribes who were the counterpart of modern stenotypists. It was not very difficult to take Genesis I as a factual account of God's creative activity—even if it involved shutting one's eyes to the fact that Genesis II gave another outline quite incompatible with that which preceded it. There are some people to-day who still believe that the authority of Genesis I in matters of scientific fact may not be questioned, and that to talk in terms of such ideas as the evolution of life is just blasphemy. I have already suggested that this attitude seems to me to be a wrong one, if only because it inevitably involves a refusal even to contemplate the vast amount of evidence carefully compiled by biologists, geologists, palaeontologists, embryologists, and other varieties of highly skilled workers over more than a century. Is it really conceivable that all these people can be entirely at fault over matters of fact, or that they are removed from the rest of mankind in that their strivings after truth inevitably lead them into error?

It is sometimes said that the evolution of life cannot be proved either; and this is of course true. But nor can the execution of Charles I—at least, not to the satisfaction of any person who bluntly insists that the parliamentary records have been cooked and that all the contemporary accounts were written by liars—yet there is really no reason at all to believe that it did not happen. And the same is true of the theory of evolution, for the belief of scientists that living things have changed and that life has unfolded or evolved over some 10 million centuries is based on a careful study of the similarities between organisms and of the fossil remains documented in strata all over the world. A biologist may very reasonably throw out a challenge to the fundamentalists by pointing out that the mere finding of one single specimen in the wrong layer of sedimentary rock would cause the whole theory to collapse like a house of cards, yet such a find has never been made. On the contrary, every fresh quarrying operation and each new sinking of a mine shaft brings to light just such specimens as could be forecast on the basis of the theory of evolution, and the evidence of the rocks not only remains unshaken but is reinforced. No alternative doctrine of the creation of man can be taken seriously into account unless it can give a reasonable explanation of this reliability of the record written in the Earth's crust.

I think that the refusal of some Christians to face the certainty of evolution (as opposed to some of the wilder romancings in the theories connected with it) is in part emotional and in part due to misconceptions about such writings as are included in Genesis. Fortunately we now know much about the sources of Genesis I to II, and painstaking research has disentangled the various strands of very different date from which the composite whole was compiled. We know, too, that the outlines of the book of Genesis date from the time when Israel was apparently well established in the promised land, and that its purpose was to provide a survey of the past which was in keeping with what the Israelite knew from his own experience of such things as the care of God, the traditionally accepted rights and wrongs of personal conduct, and the sheer existence of failure and evil—quite apart from minor phenomena such as rain and rainbows. The material chosen to form the framework was not just invented on the spur of the moment but culled from tradition and legend and accounts handed down (no doubt with occasional embellishment) from generation to generation, and from song and poetry also. Later, the priests carried out considerable editing, and they added other material which in some respects was more mature and represented the results of centuries of careful thought. Amongst these additions was the creation story with which the Bible opens. This is far more detailed and more scientific than the older Garden of Eden tale that immediately follows it, which is concerned more with the origin of evil than with the universe—though even this earlier account is delightfully modern in the way in which it portrays men as blaming their failures on women, and the women in passing the responsibility to the serpent, whether the reptile in question be Satan, a smooth second-hand motor-dealer, or some convenient psychological concept such as " libido."

Genesis is thus a collection of writings of very different dates and origins, some of them being sagas enshrining germs of historical truth, others unembroidered history, and still others parable or legend with a moral attached. Yet this is not all, for Genesis I certainly represents a very gallant and quite successful attempt to integrate the limited factual knowledge of the time with the insight of the writers into the nature of God as revealed both in his dealings with man and in the sheer magnificence of the universe. That the detail does not necessarily square with modern knowledge is hardly surprising, for although the Bible may be the " word of God " it is certainly not the transcript of a live broadcast from the palace of the deity. It was written by men as surely as Darwin's *Origin of Species* was the work of human hand and mind, and however devotedly the Old Testament authors strove to open their hearts and minds to the knowledge of God their efforts, like our own, were handicapped by the sheer limitations of human thought and experience, and what they wrote inevitably fell short of complete understanding—particularly where they were concerned with facts of physics and biology which are only known to us as a result of centuries of experiment and research. Darwin was able to take into account the world-wide discoveries and observations of other men whose whole lives had been spent in cataloguing creatures ranging from fleas to elephants. He was situated far down the line of the great tradition of human learning and endeavour, whereas the unknown author who wrote the Genesis account of creation some twenty-five centuries ago was at a dis-advantage. He could only state a hypothesis which appeared to fit the facts, and there was no accumulation of detailed study and human experience against which to check it.

An example may make this difference clearer. All the writers of the Old Testament regarded the Earth as a flat plate, and they sometimes referred to the pillars which were supposed to support it. To-day we know that the Earth is roughly spherical, and that it does not stand on legs like a billiard table. But we have only *known* this for certain since Magellan sailed round the globe, although later achievements in technology have made it possible to demonstrate the roundness of the world in many other ways. A midday phone call from London to Singapore will reveal that the sun is already setting in Malaya, whilst another to Chicago will confirm that in Illinois the dawn is just beginning to break. If further evidence is wanted it is to be had in the photographs taken from space rockets, in which the curving of the Earth's surface can at once be seen.

The cosmologists of the Old Testament had no telephones and space rockets, nor had they circumnavigated the globe. In describing the architecture of the universe they had to make deductions from what they could actually see, and Genesis I is an admirably reasonable account of what can still be seen to-day by any person who stands on a hillside and surveys the starry sky and the Earth below it. The firmament, that strange crystal dome vaulting over the sky and holding the stars in position, is as visible now as it was then, and the only difference is that we now know that it is not really there at all. But we only know this as a result of the work of astronomers from Tycho Brahe to Fred Hoyle, and because scientists have invented telescopes, radio-telescopes, spectrographs, and all manner of highly ingenious appliances which have enabled them to see beyond appearances at least to some glimmerings of reality.

The same is true of the creation of living things. There was no reason to think in terms other than those of a special creation of the comparatively few species known to the inhabitants of the Middle East until measurements of sediments and an examination of strata laid bare in the quarrying and mining operations of the Industrial Revolution suggested a very different story. The author of Genesis I formulated a perfectly sound scheme of things on the basis of the restricted data available, and if we can now describe things differently it is only because we are farther down the line of the tradition of knowledge and have technical aids of which he could never have dreamed. It is perfectly reasonable to regard his account as that of a scientist propounding a tentative theory, even if he may (for all we know) have thought of his description as much more than tentative—as scientists in our own day are equally inclined to do.

Yet the Genesis writer was not just a man giving a factual description to the best of his ability. He was a poet too, and above all he was fully alive to the goodness and beauty and power of the creation, and he saw it all as a reflection of the creator. He saw man as made " in the image " of God, reflecting however dimly the qualities of his maker and deliberately created to play his part in the management of the world by subjecting nature to his own rule, having dominion over it, not as an exploiter but as an administrator carrying out the purposes of his master. And it is interesting to note that whereas some Christians have regarded the sheer existence of sex in humans as being an evil thing made by a creator who should really have known better or who was not fully awake to the dangerous consequences of such an ingenious device, the Hebrew writer had no such doubts about the wisdom of God in making not just humans but men and women.

The biblical creation stories, then, can be regarded as brilliant attempts to account for things as they were and to interpret them in terms of the power and purpose of God. To-day we can give detailed descriptions which are very different, and which may contain no reference at all to the relationship of the universe to a deity. And this, even if it may be the cause of misunderstandings, is perhaps as it should be. Science is an analysis of phenomena in terms only of measurement and of immediate cause and effect. A scientist may be as conscious as a theologian of the power and goodness, the beauty and mystery and purpose which fill the interstellar vastness or the teeming life within a drop of pond water, but it is not his business *as a scientist* to comment upon it. He has his own carefully delineated methods of revealing one particular aspect of truth, and it is the mechanisms alone which are his concern. His whole method of approach is streamlined to analyse only this one aspect of his subject, but this does not mean either that other aspects do not exist, or even that he is necessarily unaware of them. In much the same way a landscape painter may be very conscious of the rustlings of the breeze in the trees which he is painting, but he does not draw a sound-track round the edge of his canvas to remind us that he is not deaf.

This, I think, is insufficiently explained to those who learn science at school or study it at the university, or watch from their own armchairs some of the astonishing discoveries of modern science brought to them in the glow of the television screen. To-day we can give a description of the universe, or of the succession of living creatures on the earth, which is technically far more accurate than that of the Genesis compilers and surely it would be a poor reflection upon the human mind if in twenty-five centuries it had not managed to discover some new details of these things—but these descriptions are only in strictly physical or biological terms, and they make no mention of purpose or of God as the originator and creator. On the other hand, the older accounts are now known to be wrong in many matters of fact, and because these older, inaccurate theories tied the creation to God and the newer, more precise ones do not, it is often assumed that the idea of God is in itself either irrelevant or an old-fashioned illusion like the firmament. I suspect that a misunderstanding of this kind may account for the frequent astonishment of those who suddenly discover that some highly reputable man of science is at the same time a very sincere and well-informed Christian. Yet there is not in reality much less reason why a scientist should be a Christian than that a successful painter or surgeon or builder should be.

I have said " *not much less reason* " deliberately, because there is of course a difference. A scientist may have to face challenges to his faith which are unknown to other people; or, if he has no particular faith to start with he may easily come to be so concerned with causal " how " mechanisms that he may overlook the very existence of other and quite different relationships which lie outside his professional orbit. If Kinsey overlooked love as a factor in marriage, it was not necessarily because he thought it did not exist, but more probably because of his concentration on immediate causes which could be treated statistically and were more precisely definable.

Nowadays we are nearly all of us scientists at least to the extent of being aware of the broad outlines of the main scientific theories, and if the Christian finds that these theories contain no reference to God he should not be surprised, for science is only telling him how things are arranged and constituted and is not concerned with the sheer fact of their existence at all. Yet from time to time some scientific discovery or theory will appear to imply a contradiction of a particular point of faith, and when this is the case the honest Christian must try to discover whether the contradiction is a real one, or whether his faith may need revision—and whether such a revision would bring fresh insight or would conflict uncompromisingly with his own experience and with that of others.

VIII

THE NATURE OF LIFE

The real problem for the Christian in an age of science lies very much deeper than arguing the toss about the origin of the solar system, or whether the Earth and its contents were made in seven days or in 4000 million years, and whether or not man is closely related to apes. These minor points may certainly trouble children, but to thinking Christians they should present no difficulty which cannot be overcome by half a minute of quiet reflection. It is more in the actual mechanics of evolution that bewilderment may seem to lie, for purpose in the world of nature as a whole, and in the origin of man in particular, has no place whatsoever in evolutionary theory; more than that, the concept may appear to imply that the whole of existence is based on a complete absence of all sense and purpose.

To the Christian, man is a specially designed creature, living in a much wider sense than the blade of grass or the bed-bug, because he mirrors (however dimly) the more fundamental aspects of his creator. God can speak and man can answer—even though, as the earliest Genesis selection so appropriately points out, he is rather more inclined to hide in the shrubbery and pretend he has not heard. Yet to the same person in his capacity as a student of biology, man appears to be nothing but an assemblage of chapter upon chapter of accidents, and might perhaps be described by the symbol r^n, where r is a coefficient of randomness. In the first place the mere existence of the Earth, whether born of a supernova explosion or formed by a near collision of two stars or by any other means at all, appears to have been sheer chance. It so happened that the Earth ended up in a position where it was neither too hot nor too cold, and was of just the right size to hold down an atmosphere containing oxygen and water without a host of undesirable companion substances, and thus have all the very special characteristics needed for the complex chemical processes involved in life; and although it may be natural to see in all this the hand of God, the fact remains that science explains it all in terms of purely random events.

On top of this comes the postulated chance origin of life already mentioned in an earlier chapter, and the evolution of countless successive forms as each chance variation was played upon by the ever-shifting physical and ecological background. Climate changed, humidity and temperature varied, the saltness of the sea and the extent of land masses, oceans, mud and mountains, were altered throughout vast periods of time by the interaction of such inexorable and soulless variables as the inclination of the Earth's axis, the contraction or expansion of its orbit, and the proximity of the Sun to the centre of the ellipse. Sunspots and other unpredictable phenomena played their part too, and ice ages, dry spells, warm dinosaurian swamps and dusty deserts swept over areas of our planet, each succeeding state having its origin in nothing more than random combinations of random events, and ensuring the development and survival or decay and extinction of countless varieties of creatures, according to whether they happened to be suitable to their surroundings.

"Natural Selection" and "Survival of the Fittest"—whether these were the only factors involved in evolutionary succession, or whether the main lines of advance were laid down in spite of them and in actual defiance of chance, as certain biologists have suggested, they indubitably had at least a caretaker rôle to play, and variations came and went in steps with changes in the environment. What is more, the variations themselves upon which selection could work appear to have had their origin in gene mutations and random mix-ups of chromosomes which make their presence known to the observer by visible effects (often delayed for many generations) in the creatures concerned. The white forelock of Harry Hotspur's son, faithfully transmitted through five centuries of births, marriages, and deaths to our present day, can be shown to have been caused by a single gene mutation. The "sport" or colour variant in a bed of red dahlias in a park owes its special hue to a mutation too, and so does the *Drosophila* fly with four joints instead of five in its legs. The blackness of a black cat, the whiteness of the white deer, even perhaps the mathematical ability of a research physicist—all these are hereditary variations, the external manifestations of gene mutations. And a mutation is no more than a slight change in the arrangement of a maze of atoms within a small grouping at some particular point of a giant molecule which constitutes the vital part of a chromosome, the mechanical basis of inheritance.

The change in the phenotype (or outward manifestation of a particular collection of genes) is random too. There seems no *reason* why the alternative to light or dark-brown human hair should be white and not vermilion with yellow spots, not why the melanic form of the peppered moth which has proved so successful in the Black Country should be blackish—the fact that if it had been of any other hue it could not have won through to become relatively abundant is not a demonstration of purposeful design but just one more example of the inexorable efficiency of Natural Selection in promoting chance variations.

Mutations are not only random in their effects, but in their origin too. Not all the causes of genetic change have yet been discovered, but at least we know that something sudden and unexpected must shake up the atoms and throw them into an isomeric form of molecule, from which they sometimes jump back again. Cosmic rays and "natural" radioactivity certainly provide some of the necessary tickles, and it can hardly be described as anything but chance if such a nuclear bullet should strike one particular group on one particular chromosome which is going to be successful in the shufflings which take place in the formation of the sex cells and reach the particular egg or sperm cell which is to provide half the heredity of an individual in the next generation. Yet this is probably the way in which the heir to the throne of Spain came to be a haemophilic, and it may be no exaggeration to say that had the chair in which

Queen Victoria's mother was doing her needlework only been placed one ten-thousandth of an inch farther from the table the mutation would not have occurred, and her great-grandson would have been able to shave without embarrassment or danger instead of being obliged to have a bottle of coagulant within arm's reach in the bathroom.

We are not even yet at the end of the catalogue of chances, for in the course of evolution the success of one creature depended to a certain extent upon the random changes in others. Nature is intricately linked in this way, and Darwin himself cited an example in a correlation between the number of cats and the abundance of the wild pansy or heartsease (*Viola tricolor.*) At first sight a connection between two such unrelated organisms might seem most improbable, but in fact the cats are the enemies of field mice, which alone burrow into and destroy the nests of bumble-bees, which are the particular insect which visit the heartsease and ensure its fertilisation by carrying the pollen from flower to flower. More cats (or perhaps more owls) means less mice, fewer mice means more young bumbles, and more bumbles ensures a more widespread fertilisation of heartsease.

Few scientists would suggest that we know all there is to be known about the origin and development of life, but that is not to say that we only have to wait for a decade or two for new discoveries to show evolutionary theory politely out of the door. Odds and ends of loose threads will certainly be tied up, but evolution as such is so firmly established on observed facts that it is safe to say that it is with us for ever, whether we like it or not. And personally I admit to liking it, for whatever difficulties it raises I share the view of Charles Darwin himself that " When I view all the beings not as special creations, but as lineal descendants of some few beings which lived long before the first bed of the Silurian system was deposited, they seem to me to become ennobled. . . . There is grandeur in this view of life, with its several powers, having been originally breathed by the Creator into a few forms or into one." The individual person, whether it be myself or someone I love, or some political schemer whom I loathe, is no longer a capricious toy of the creator, but part of the very stuff of the universe. Orion and the Pleiades are no longer remote and terrifying in their immensity; they have a real affinity with mankind and I can look up at them with humble but brotherly affection.

Yet merely to find evolution fascinating and to draw from it a sense of unity with the whole of the creation is not to exorcise its difficulties, for the fact remains that what *we* can only think of as randomness and accident runs right through the whole background to our existence. What then is the Christian to think of it all? How is he to square this apparently purposeless mechanism with his essential belief in a God who is all powerful and loving and purposeful? Once again the temptation to fundamentalism rears its alluring head, and there is no doubt that the simplest course would be to throw in one's hand and refuse to consider the facts at all. It is no coincidence that the reactionary and fundamentalist sects are continually gaining in numerical strength at a time when science is leaping from one great discovery to another, but Christians would do well to recall the reaction of Christ to this same temptation. Whatever else were the temptations with which he had to wrestle before he began his ministry, one of them was directly concerned with the matter of taking refuge in a literal interpretation of the scriptures. The gospel gives us the story in delightful form, picturing the devil as saying to Jesus, "Why don't you take scripture at its face value? Doesn't it say that God will see that his angels take care that the man who trusts in him will not even sprain his ankle? Well then, try it out. Jump over this parapet and see what happens!"

If refuge in literalism is rejected as the flight from reason and responsibility which it certainly is, then several other choices remain. For instance, one may assure oneself that the workings of nature in natural selection take care of the general running of the universe, but that God can and does intervene from time to time to slant events in the particular direction which is in accordance with his will. This notion is an attractive one, but I think that it must inevitably lead to a concept of God which falls short of the Christian ideal. God is certainly regarded as almighty in the sense that he can interfere and change the course of events, but he can hardly be thought of as the Father of all things whose dominion extends over everything except the wilful denials and rebellious spirit of mankind. Nor is he any longer the sustainer of the universe; on the contrary, the universe goes its own chancy way until the creator decides that the time is ripe to fix another supernova explosion or to equip the first mammals with fur.

Alternatively one may think of God as the all-wise and far-seeing being who was so expert in physics and chemistry that he was able right at the start and many billions of years ago to frame the laws of nature with such precision that everything would turn out just right. The value of gravity was calculated so neatly and to so many decimal places that the Earth was inevitably formed in the right position and came to swing through an orbit at just the best possible distance from the Sun. It inevitably became endowed with its essential qualities, and the whole rig of the solar system was such that our climate would change in just the right way to act upon the mutations which the deity's expert knowledge of nucleo-proteins foresaw as developing just when required. Such a God would well be omniscient but he would not be a sustainer of the universe; nor is it at all obvious why he should have any further interest in his creation. Without even needing to oil the wheels, he might be no more than a master mechanic who constructed a brilliant piece of machinery and then left it to run its course alone and untended. This again is hardly a concept which can satisfy the Christian, with his insistence that God is alive, ever present, and approachable. The world could get along just as well without him if he were no more than a brilliant theoretical physicist and technician.

A variation on this idea of God as an expert mechanic might well be that he did indeed draw up the laws of physics and chemistry with the result that a universe was set in motion which looked after itself well enough on the material side alone, but that the eventual development of man as a sentient being demanded that God should once again get to work. With creatures now roaming about on two legs, equipped with good brains and having the capacity to be dimly aware of their creator, it was necessary for God to have dealings with them in a number of ways, culminating in a concrete exhibition of his own nature in Christ so that men would realise where they stood. This idea is somewhat more satisfactory, but it is not without its difficulties—for example, it does not need the continual presence of God throughout existence, except in so far as he is represented by the operation of his machinery.

Perhaps our troubles stem less from evolution than from the Genesis compilers, whose words are breathed into our ears in early childhood, and who found it necessary to present God to the Israelites in very anthropomorphic form as a kind of superman " somewhere up there." This filled the bill well enough for people whose prime concerns were with their history and destiny, but it is not adequate for those of us who live in an era when even the " up there " has vanished in the smoke of relativity.

Yet this factual inadequacy of the Genesis concepts, which we often assume to be a discovery of our own scientific and enlightened age, is nothing new. Right at the start of the Christian era the older teaching had to be reinterpreted, and in the opening verses of St. John's Gospel the vision of a creator was recast with far greater insight—a fact which seems often to be overlooked. And I think that the problem for the Christian of facing up to the universe has never been better solved than in these verses of St. John. It may be easier to visualise the creation in the Genesis terms of God making an *external* universe and then fitting it out with physical properties and with living creatures all separately and ingeniously designed, but St. John's realisation that the creation was *internal*— that is, that the universe itself was a part of God—is the thing that really matters. Every Christmas these words pour from the radio in the course of the carol services and there must be few people who are not deeply moved by their beauty; but the real brilliance of what they say may often drift past unapprehended—perhaps because of the familiarity of the verses themselves. Yet it seems to me that they contain the solution of all the riddles which scientific discovery has posed, for an understanding of the creation is not a matter of wondering how God knew that the dinosaurs would be a dead letter, or whether he intervened to make man's ancestors descend from the trees, but lies in realising that in giving us so much information about the mechanisms of the universe science is helping us to appreciate one tiny aspect of God's anatomy.

I think it is only within this concept that we begin to comprehend something of the nature of life itself. The absolute wonder of life, the mere fact that atoms and molecules can be strung together in such configurations that the resulting complex can live and reproduce, is in itself so astounding that it is not unnatural that Christians should regard life itself as a kind of essence of God breathed into inanimate matter. Many people feel instinctively that man could never make even the simplest organism or virus, and they are quite certain too that the original formation of life on our planet was an occasion when God suddenly intervened to impart some kind of vital spark. When geophysicists and oceanographers talk of life having probably " arisen " from the mere collisions of molecules of gases in the atmosphere or the primeval seas, under the influence of light or lightning, many Christians feel that such a theory is almost blasphemous because it would seem finally to do away with any need for a creator.

But we must face the facts, some of which are at first glance rather surprising. In the experiments of Miller and others a mixture of methane and ammonia and water and hydrogen—the same simple materials as we may fairly assume were present in the atmosphere of those distant ages—when placed in a sealed flask and subjected to nothing more than electrical discharges has actually produced amino-acids identical with those from which the sacrosanct proteins of living things are built up. Nor can the suggestion that the vital enzymes could simply have arisen when volcanic lava ran into the sea be seen any longer as sheer romance, for at temperatures of only two or three hundred degrees centigrade various simple molecules have already been shown to join up into more complex arrangements, and the theory that carbon dioxide and water alone, in the presence of sunlight and magnetic ore, might yield living chemicals now seems very reasonable indeed. For all we know, life may be " arising " on our own planet and elsewhere in the universe in some such simple way, at this very moment.

Personally I regret that such discoveries should upset people. It will be surprising if within a decade or two a step forward has not been taken from Miller's experiment to the production of real live self-reproducing molecules. To some it will then seem that the last rampart has fallen of the fortress over which they have despairingly kept flying the standard of God's unique activity as a creator, but I think that such discoveries should rather help us to get rid of the deadweight of the notion that there is a " dead " universe into which God can breathe the breath of life when the occasion happens to be suitable, and should enable us to realise as we surely ought that the whole universe is nothing but life in the making. From end to end it is absolutely pregnant with the idea of life—with the almost incredible possibility that its protons and neutrons and radiations can form up and develop into such complex organisms as ourselves, creatures who can think and speculate about the creation itself, made though we are of nothing but particles of energy whirling in their submicroscopic orbits.

I hope that I shall see the day when some biochemist receives a Nobel Prize for the first " synthesis " of life. There may then be much talk of sacrilegious activity in aping the work of the creator, but I would like to think that the same scientist will receive telegraphed congratulations rather than abuse from the Christian Churches. For all that he will have done is to demonstrate that the very stuff of the universe is not dead and mechanical, but vibrant from end to end with the germs of awareness of God, of which to be alive is an essential requirement. That the materials of the rocks can be melted and refined and cast and machined into automobiles and television sets is wonderful enough; but if the air which rustles the leaves of the trees and the water which falls from the heavy clouds beneath a sky torn by the vivid discharge of lightning are loaded with the possibility of giving rise to the mind of man as a reflection of the love of God, then this is surely something of which we are not sufficiently aware. It is a sad consideration that although we have had the opening words of St. John's Gospel for centuries it may still need the work of biochemists to shake us into an honest realisation of their truth.

Yet in some ways the whole of the scientific picture, though majestic and exciting, is not really essential, for what primarily concerns the Christian in his faith is the purpose of God in the relationship of devotion and responsibility between man and his creator. To this, supernovae and mutations, cosmic rays and evolutionary pressure, are neither here nor there, for the knowledge of the relationship is derived from quite different sources—from personal experience to a limited extent, but mainly from the authority of Christ.

This at once raises the question whether the authority of Christ is worth anything at all. The New Testament consists only of a handful of much-copied manuscripts of the pre-scientific age, larded with tales of a rather improbable nature, and however much we might like to accept what they tell us it is reasonable to consider whether they have any more valid claim upon our attention than the queer speculations of the alchemists as to the true nature of the elements.

IX

THE HISTORICAL JESUS

Although a belief in an active creator is necessary to any Christian, such a matter has no actual and direct bearing upon the centre and pivot of all Christian faith—the life of Christ himself. To some, the life of Christ is all that matters and one sometimes hears it said that all that is necessary for the Christian is an acceptance of the *person* of Christ, but unless the word " person " is interpreted very broadly indeed I do not think this is true. It is like saying that all one needs in a motor-car is an internal combustion engine. Certainly the engine is the really distinctive thing about a car as compared with a horse-gig, but the car still needs a chassis, and wheels, and other things besides. Without these, the engine would be best lodged in a scrapyard, or (if it has particularly quaint and historic mechanisms) in a museum; and the same applies to a Christianity so restricted that it cannot embrace the whole of one's knowledge. A faith which merely regarded Christ as a person who was the perfect example of virtues and values and who went around exhorting men to strive to transform a world which was in essence beyond control and devoid of purpose would certainly not satisfy me.

But if a Christian has somehow to come to terms with the universe and try to see however dimly its relation to a creator, this in itself provides no basis for a proper faith. At best it can do little more than give one a conviction that however strangely things may appear they will work out right enough in the end. The universe and life itself are only the necessary stage on which the life of the individual is played, and to the Christian that life only makes sense within his personal knowledge of Christ.

What any Christian knows about Christ comes from three sources. There is the tradition and recorded experience of previous generations, which includes the teaching of the Church, and this corresponds very much to what a modern physicist or biologist receives in the way of scientific theory and laws from scientists who have gone before; and just as a scientist will try to check this information so far as he has any doubts about it, so a Christian will not necessarily accept uncritically all that stems from theological treatises and sermons and conferences of years gone by. It may be thought that doctrine and tradition are much less precise than scientific theory, if only because the Roman Church has certain dogmas which are quite different from the traditions of other denominations; indeed, the mere variety of Christian teaching may suggest that the whole of it is suspect. Yet very much the same is found in science. Biology has its Darwinians and Lamarckians, psychology its Freudians and Jungians and Adlerians. The views of these schools of thought are very different, but that does not mean that biology and psychology are nonsense. In doctrine as well as in scientific theory there is an effort to get at the truth, however varied the starting-points from which one may begin the search.

Besides doctrine the Christian, like the scientist, has his own actual experience, and for the Christian this consists in his intimate personal relationship as an individual with what he calls "the living Christ"—an odd-enough term, one might think, to apply to an intangible aftermath of a man who lived nineteen centuries ago, but really no stranger than what a scientist calls the "reliability of chance." The laws of chance (an extraordinary contradiction in terms) prove reliable enough to carry predictions which turn out correctly, and so does the personal relationship with a living person who died 1900 years ago.

Basically, however, the Christian stakes his faith on his acceptance of Christ as a genuine figure of history, a man just as real and authentic as the famous, if minor, Roman official Pontius Pilate who happened to be his contemporary. If the figure of Jesus is mythical, or even grossly distorted, then Christianity has no claim whatsoever upon our attention—just as chemistry would be a remarkably dead duck if the elements in their free states did not really exist at all.

Now the concept of Jesus as a historical figure rests almost entirely on the New Testament. Pagan or non-Christian works of the time may here and there give a passing reference to disturbances in Judaea or reveal that the Roman emperors used the stubborn followers of an executed villager as food for the wild beasts in the fun and games of the arena, but it is in the New Testament alone that Jesus is portrayed in any detail, and on the writings contained in it the Christian stakes everything—sometimes life itself. The question for those who live in a modern age is whether it is at all reasonable to stake anything on the veracity of rather sketchy documents of such great age, when other ancient texts are obviously very far removed from being compendiums of truth. For example, nobody could take all the events of the *Odyssey* seriously, nor those of the sagas of Scandinavia or the Nibelungen tales of Germany. These medieval works may be of great interest or merit from a literary point of view, but they could never be regarded as unembroidered accounts of real happenings, and yet the sagas are a thousand years more modern than the gospels. Why then should the Christian regard the New Testament as authoritative, and not just as a series of writings in which ideas and ideals are dressed up and put into the mouths of a character either invented for the purpose, or suitably adapted by elaboration from a genuine person who was a somewhat original and revolutionary idealist, but who has no greater claim to his allegiance than any other philosopher or teacher or dreamer?

To grow up accepting without question that the New Testament record is fact and not fiction is comfortable, but it is not always easy for the man or woman in a scientific age to do so. Nor is it possible to draw on anything much in the way of external evidence which might directly confirm what the New Testament relates of the life of Christ. This is not really at all surprising, for the account is set in an era very different from our own, an age in which the sheer cataloguing of facts important and unimportant had not been begun. Writing was laborious, printing lay more than a thousand years ahead, and so there was not the wealth of incidental confirmatory record which is continually being produced to-day. For example, if a student of local history were to find that in his locality there was a tradition that three centuries ago a local boy had run away to sea and had returned home with a fortune to build a great manor house (since pulled down without trace), and that he had married a certain young lady from the neighbouring county and sent his son to Eton, and that this son had later become ambassador at the court of the United Provinces, each of these facts could almost certainly be confirmed over and over again by resort to parish registers, collections of family letters, notes in official dispatches, items in the title-deeds or plans in the Land Registry and the like. Solicitors' files, dusty bundles of records in the county archives, chance references in the diaries of other people— all these would either confirm or refute the tale. But Christianity founds its beliefs on writings from a time when such cross-checking evidence just did not exist, and so it is to the New Testament itself that we have to turn for the evidence of its own authenticity. This may sound rather like asking a man of doubtful integrity whether he ever tells lies, but the situation is really rather different. A vast amount of scientific study of the New Testament texts has been undertaken, and to-day we know a surprising amount about their origins.

There are twenty-seven books in the New Testament: four gospels which purport to give us the history of Christ (or, in the case of St. John, the meaning of his ministry); one account, partly in diary form, of the events in the years immediately after the crucifixion; one prophetic work designed to assure persecuted Christians that right would nevertheless prevail in the end; and twenty-one letters of varying length, written by several different authors. All but two of these books were certainly written by Jews (St. Luke's Gospel and Acts being the possible exceptions).

The letters or epistles might seem somewhat irrelevant

as evidence, but on the contrary they are a mine of information. The Epistles to the Thessalonians are known to have been written at least a decade before the earliest of the gospels—and it would be an odd thing to write to people and make mention of a character who had not yet been invented! In fact all the letters—probably ten—which can definitely be assigned to Paul's own hand must have been written before his death in A.D. 64, and some, if not all of them, must therefore have been produced before the earliest of the gospels. But quite apart from this, the epistles contain just those touches which one would expect if the correspondent were writing of a figure with whose life he was familiar, and whose close friends and associates were known to him intimately. Thus in writing his first letter to the Corinthians Paul described the last supper in detail, not as regards the seating arrangements, but concerning what Jesus did and what he said, and if he could do so there can be only two explanations. Either he had invented the story, or he had the details from those who knew them because they were present—in other words, his information was second-hand. Yet second-hand material can be perfectly true and accurate in matter of detail. We all have information on repeated hearsay evidence, without its being erroneous, and this is particularly the case where sayings or actions are memorable. " Why don't you come up and see me some time?"—I know well enough what film star spoke those words, though I never saw or heard her, either on the screen or off it. Second-hand evidence may not be accepted in British courts, but that does not mean that it is necessarily mistaken.

If Paul was indeed mistaken in what he related, or if for reasons of his own he had just invented it, one can hardly imagine that he could have deceived people successfully about the actions and sayings of a Jesus who had been alive only twenty years earlier. What he alleged would have been quickly and energetically corrected, and his fantasies would have been torn to pieces by any one of the hundreds of people among his contemporaries who could remember with the greatest vividness Christ's actions and words during his brief dramatic years of public ministry. Yet we have no apocryphal or other epistles from the other apostles warning the Corinthians, Galatians, Romans, and Ephesians of the early churches not to believe what this crafty, romancing, letter-writing theologian Paul had been telling them. Of course one might suggest that the censorship of the early Church energetically collected them and destroyed them without trace or record, but this does not seem credible. It is surely much more reasonable to suppose that such details of the life of Jesus as appear in the numerous epistles went unchallenged because they were known to be correct.

Yet if the epistles thoroughly confirm the gospels, it is from the gospels themselves that the Christian derives his knowledge of the historical figure of Jesus. I do not wish to go into the detail of the brilliant research which has been done on the origin of these four books and the comparative study of their texts, for any Christian should know that St. Mark is the earliest, written about A.D. 65-70 and that it was based on the direct recollections and oft-repeated accounts of Peter and other early missionaries. Mark was at times Paul's personal travelling companion, and he made it his job to set down what was known of Jesus before all those who had first-hand information had died. St. Luke and St. Matthew were written later and each used St. Mark's Gospel as a source, but their authors also drew on another account called "Q" (for *Quelle*, German for source) which has never been found but which was an eye-witness account, written perhaps by Matthew the tax-collector. So it is fair to describe these three gospels as consisting of both first-hand and second-hand material interwoven, and with occasional later insertions which do not concern us here.

But are the gospels true? If none of them was written until a third of a century after the death of their central figure it may seem reasonable to wonder whether they are factual, and whether the events recorded in St. Matthew can sensibly be accepted as anything more than legend. Yet our newspapers often carry obituary notices containing

references to incidents in the youth of the person who has
died, contributed by some person who remembers him
very clearly from an early and intimate friendship, but
whose association with him ceased forty or fifty years ago.
Attitudes of mind, certain particular sayings, and actions on
important occasions persist permanently in the memory of
others throughout their lives. The gospels are recollections,
told at first- and second-hand, of men and women who
were there at the time and knew Jesus intimately. The
fact that they did not write down the day-to-day events
before they retired to bed each night is no reason for doubt-
ing the accuracy of what they could recall.

If we consider what would be remembered in the way
of minor detail as the years slipped by, we can well imagine
that some things would be remembered more precisely than
others, and that the particular way of life and interests
of those who handed on the information to the writers
would very much determine the kind of detail which they
remembered vividly. And a glance at the gospels shows
at once that certain little items of fact which in themselves
were of no importance in presenting the character of Jesus
had imprinted themselves on the observers. To us, nineteen centuries later, these incidentals ring astonishingly
true. It is natural enough that Peter the boat-owner and
lake fisherman would recall quite unselfconsciously any
details which had a particular connection with his trade,
and that in passing on his recollections to Mark and others
he would retail them as a matter of course. We can see
that he did so, and when in St. Mark we come upon his
pieces of nautical information they strike us most forcibly
as being just such things as a man of his particular trade
would mention in his preaching or in handing on his vivid
recollections of the incidents, whereas other and less nautic-
ally minded witnesses would have omitted them, not just
as irrelevant but because they had not even noticed them.
What were the Zebedee brothers doing when Jesus came
upon them? The matter is of no direct importance to
the reader of the gospel, who is concerned with Jesus's
" Follow me," yet Peter remembered as any seaman would

that they were mending their nets aboard their father's
ship, and that they left the paid hands to carry on. And in
the tale of the storm on the lake the real point is the teaching of Jesus on the matter of faith, yet Peter recalled just
where Jesus was sleeping in the boat, and that he was
stretched out on a cushion in the stern—the kind of detail
which would never be invented by a deceitful witness or a
romancing scribe.

But apart from such details, what would any man reliably
remember of an acquaintance of many years before, whether
an intimate friend of long standing or a person whom
he had known at greater distance? This is a question
which anyone can answer from his own experience. It is
the attitudes of mind which stand out, reinforced perhaps
by particular words or favourite expressions and sometimes
by a characteristic action.

Some time ago I received a letter from a German scientist
in which he said that he was compiling an appreciation
of the life of Professor Spemann, the biologist who received
a Nobel Prize for his discovery of the organisation centre
of a developing embryo, and who died in 1941. He was
therefore approaching a number of people, including
myself, who had studied in Spemann's institute in Freiburg
many years before, and inviting them to send any observations and recollections of the professor. It was twenty
years since I had spent a few brief months in Spemann's
laboratory, and I had never been engaged with him on his
own particular researches, yet I could recall him very
clearly. I remembered the quiet and gentle if rather
troubled face, and the broad forehead with the grey hair
brushed somewhat back. I could call to mind the slow and
soft southern voice, and I remembered that Spemann
usually wore a fawn cardigan—a fact of no importance at
all. Of course these details were all true enough but I did
not record them, for they were of no help in portraying
Spemann as an individual.

But I remembered other things too, and particularly the
clear and cold spring evening on which I climbed up to
his house on the hillside above the city to take my leave

before returning to England. He sat at his desk, leaning back in his chair with the tips of his fingers together, and for a while we talked of things of no particular importance. Indeed I cannot remember what we talked about, except that he explained that the *Daphne mezereum* which grew in a certain wood was of a deeper bluish purple because of the lime content in the soil (a thing which stuck in my memory only because I happened to be interested in wild flowers).

After a while Spemann rose without a word and drew back the long curtain of dark velvet from in front of the window. He gazed out in silence for a moment and then beckoned me over. Below the house the ground fell away to the plain at the foot of the Black Forest, and the lights of Freiburg sparkled in the clear air of the spring night. Over to the left the smoke from the locomotives shone as a thin haze in the glare of the lamps of the railway yards, but ahead the whole city lay mapped in dotted lines of light. To the right the forest rose up darkly, with only a gleam from the café on the Schlossberg above the cathedral. We stood for perhaps a minute, looking out over the scene towards where the lights faded away in the distance of the Rhine plain. Then Spemann spoke.

"You will never see that again," he said in his gentle voice. And then, after a pause, "It is too late." He took the curtain and pulled it deliberately across the window, shutting out the glimmer of the city he loved. "Within ten years it will all be destroyed. . . ."

In setting down the memory of that evening for the scientist who had written to ask for my recollections of Spemann I was merely recalling the one event which I particularly remembered, and no doubt it was quite in keeping with the character of Spemann as given in much greater detail by those who knew him much more intimately than I did. That I could recall the scene is hardly surprising, for I would have been unable to forget the professor's simple and despairing words even if they had not proved so prophetic when eight years later Freiburg was almost entirely destroyed in an air-raid. But it was not just the words which were so indelibly imprinted on my memory. It was Spemann's attitude to international enmities, and even more than that his absolute conviction that already, several years before 1939, the threshold into destruction had been crossed, and that nothing could avert the consequences of the folly that had been.

How very understandable it is that Peter and Matthew, and any others among the lifetime companions of Jesus who contributed their recollections to the general tradition of knowledge, could not have forgotten his actions, and his attitudes towards the problems of the day (such as the question of paying taxes to Rome). We can hardly imagine them at a loss to recall the words he used when he drove the traders out of the temple, or invited any man who considered himself sinless to fling the first stone at the adulteress whom the respectable citizens had dragged in front of him. The gospels are full from end to end with deeds and attitudes which are as much in character as they are beyond the possibility of invention, and with short sayings which, once heard, could not possibly have been forgotten. "Suffer the little children to come unto me." "Go, and sin no more." "The maid is not dead, but sleepeth." "Even Solomon in all his glory . . ." No doubt Jesus said many things during the course of his public ministry, but simple and direct words such as these could not easily be forgotten by his companions, and if there are so many of them in the gospel narratives this in itself is a very strong indication that they are what they are portrayed to be— the direct and unforgettable words of Christ himself.

Actual remembrance of what Jesus taught must have been greatly aided by the way in which he tied so much of what he said to the experiences of everyday life of the people. No agricultural worker could forget the parable of the sower, and even nineteen centuries later it is difficult to see a diesel tractor hauling a seed-broadcaster across the expanse of the Lincolnshire fens or the Canadian prairies without calling to mind that some will be picked up by the birds, and some will be overgrown by weeds. And in addition, Jesus was a poet. The comparison and contrast and confirmatory echo of the Hebrew poetry has been somewhat hidden because the translators of the Bible misguidedly rendered the whole narrative from end to end in prose (even when, as in the Psalms or Proverbs, the original was clearly poetry and nothing else), but the poetry is there just the same, and it must surely have been an aid to memory. Thus the comparison of the wise and foolish house-builders, once heard, would have been particularly easy to recall, with its simple lines of repetition and contrast :

Whoever hears these words of mine
                    and *obeys* them
Is like a *wise* man who built his house on *rock*.
The rain fell and the floods swelled,
The gale blew and the storm raged,
Yet *it did not fall*!—for it was built on rock.

Whoever hears these sayings of mine
                    and *disobeys* them,
Is like a foolish man who built his house
                    on *sand*.
The rain fell and the floods swelled,
The gale blew and the storm raged,
And it fell!—and mighty was its fall.

How easily we ourselves can call to mind great lines of poetry. "The lowing herd wind slowly o'er the lea " may be language which we ourselves would hardly use, but we can recall the words better than if Gray had merely written : "The cows moo as they make their way gradually across the field."

From all this it is abundantly clear that the internal evidence for the gospels as authentic accounts of the very real life of a historical Jesus is so good that nobody who is familiar with the scientific study of the texts can doubt it. But however good the evidence for the life and teaching of Christ may be, the modern reader of the gospels inevitably finds himself wondering just how far their reliability extends, for the narrative is heavily seasoned with accounts of happenings which fall broadly within the description of "miracles," and which seem to fly in the face of all normal experience. This naturally raises the question of whether these happenings can be accepted at their face value. The teaching on the perfect way of life as outlined in the collection of poetic utterances grouped together in the Sermon on the Mount is acceptable enough; but Jesus curing lepers and feeding crowds on nothing, raising dead people to life and withering a fig-tree with a word, is something very different.

Our own experience is that we live in a world which behaves according to certain rigid "natural" laws, and miracles (in the sense of interference with these laws) tend to stick in our throats as something not easily swallowed. The Christian who believes that his faith must be intellectually acceptable is sooner or later brought face to face with the miracles of the New Testament, and forced to consider whether or not he can find for himself an attitude towards them which is consistent with his own experience of the universe and the world around him.

MIRACLES AND INTERVENTION

The New Testament presents many incidents in the life of Christ and in the years immediately after his death either frankly as miracles or in a way which confronts the reader with some apparent reversal or suspension of the normal course of the laws of nature. And if this is so, then the record is either a truthful one or it is not.

If the record is in fact correct, just as it is given, then a reader who looks at the gospels as objectively as possible and who nevertheless finds that they conflict with his own experience of the regularity of the universe might put up the following explanations :

Firstly, it is conceivable that miracles did indeed happen in biblical times just as they are recorded, but for some reason or other the world has moved on into an era in which the working of natural laws is more absolute.

Alternatively, one might suggest that the world is really miraculous in essence from end to end, and if we do not find ourselves surrounded by strange events the fault is ours. The modern generation has its nose so close over the technical grindstone that it does not see what to other generations would have been obvious—the continual appearance (under suitable circumstances) of miracles.

Or again, one can suppose that the incarnation and ministry of Christ was in itself such a transcendent miracle of divine intervention in nature that his mere presence induced a totally different order of events, which is thus correctly reported in the gospels.

On the other hand the gospel record may be false—mistaken, misinterpreted, or flatly untrue. And as this would be a serious matter to a Christian (whose faith is based on the historical Jesus if on other things also), the possible alternatives must be considered, and there are a

destruction of London—both these have been declared not only in the Press but actually from the pulpit to be miracles. I have no authority to say that they were not, and I personally have no doubt at all that if God were interested in the power politics of Europe he *could* certainly fix the winds and calms to suit, and that if he happened to think that the loss of St. Paul's would spiritually or aesthetically or for some more obscure reason have been an irretrievable loss to mankind whereas Coventry Cathedral mattered rather less because it was an aesthetic monstrosity (or perhaps a sink of theological iniquity), he *could* have arranged to save the one and let the other be blitzed. But at least we know that Jesus is on record as declaring that God does not work in this way. The people crushed by the falling tower were not necessarily the wicked; God did not prop up the wall until the righteous happened all to be out of harm's way.

Much more important, however, is the difference in nature between these alleged "miracles" and those of the New Testament, for the gospel miracles had some quite obvious point to them. It does not matter to anyone whether a statue remains standing through an earthquake or not, but it is of great moment to a cripple to be healed, or to storm-tossed fishermen in a half-swamped boat if the wind should suddenly ease. The only utterly pointless miracle recorded in the gospels seems to me to be the destruction of the fig-tree, and because this is in a class by itself we can perhaps consider it first. As a layman I do not pretend to know all the ins and outs of textual criticism, but it seems at least possible that the event recorded in St. Mark of the blasting of the fig-tree might have one of several possible explanations—and it certainly needs explanation rather than acceptance, if only because it is quite out of character with the nature of Christ, whereas most of the other miracles are entirely in keeping with his teaching. The tale as it stands is that Jesus was hungry after a journey and he saw a fig-tree in the distance. He went over to it hoping to find some fruit although, as the story tells us, it was not yet the right season. Jesus was so annoyed with the unfortunate tree that he ordered it never to bear fruit again, and when next he and his disciples passed that way the tree was dying. Peter drew his attention to it, to which (unless there is really a complete change of subject here) he merely replied, " Have faith in God "—and then went on to talk about prayer. One wonders whether there is some confusion here with another fig-tree, that of the parable recorded in St. Luke in which Jesus himself pointed out that when the tree was shooting one knew that summer was at hand. Or is it a case of misunderstanding by the eye-witnesses, and that the story was that Jesus examined the tree and saw that it was blighted or otherwise in an unhealthy condition, and that when he said, "No man eat fruit of thee hereafter for ever," he was merely stating that the tree was useless?

Or again, is this a case of a parable misinterpreted, a lesson based on the idea that a fig-tree (or a nation or a person) which bore not fruit was doomed? We know that the habit of Jesus of drawing lessons from nature led on at least one occasion to the disciples entirely misunderstanding what he said, for Mark relates how they were once ashamed and embarrassed to have thought that he was actually talking about making bread during a lake crossing when in fact (as he had to explain) he was merely using the process of baking as an illustration of the current teachings and attitudes against which they should continually be on their guard. And if on that occasion the misunderstanding was realised it is more than likely that there were other occasions on which the real significance of his words or his actions was lost on those around him, so that the version given in the gospels does not convey to us quite what it should.

We may never know the truth about the fig-tree, but we can be reasonably sure that the event cannot be accepted at its face value. It is not the actual power of blasting the tree which one rejects, but merely an action quite out of keeping with the character of Jesus as otherwise portrayed with complete consistency if one also excepts, as I think many people would, the destruction of the herd of swine. Personally I admit to every sympathy with the owners of the herd of pigs which ran over the cliff edge, and here again the destruction of the unfortunate creatures is quite out of harmony with the teaching of Jesus upon the very real value in the sight of God of even such an unprepossessing creature as a common sparrow. Both the fig-tree and the swine incidents are ones against which I myself have to place question marks—particularly the former, in which the destruction is specifically stated to have been wrought by Jesus, whereas the pigs were rather at the mercy of the devils which entered them of their own accord. Of course the incident of the swine is not without a perfectly reasonable explanation. Jesus had just cured a man who was considered to have been filled with a number of " devils," and if just afterwards a herd of pigs ran over the cliff edge and fell into the water the idea was natural enough that this was the devils going home to the " abyss," the dreadful and unspeakable place which was believed to be at the bottom of the seas, and where they belonged. However, as a child I always felt that Jesus would have stopped the poor beasts, and I am inclined to think so still.

Perhaps the best example of a miracle which might have alternative explanations is that of the feeding of the crowd on the hillside. Jesus had been addressing his thousands of hearers for some hours and eventually they became hungry. The disciples were told to get the people seated on the ground, and a boy was found who had two loaves and a few small fishes, but when Jesus had given thanks this small quantity proved more than enough to provide a full meal for the whole assemblage. At least, that is the narrative as it stands, but it might be explained in a number of ways. For instance, it could conceivably be an elaboration in simple metaphor of Jesus's lesson that he himself was the " bread of heaven " and that whoever believed him would never hunger again—having already filled his spirit with the only food that mattered. Or perhaps Jesus had preached so eloquently on the subject of loving one's neighbours (and even one's enemies) that a young lad generously pulled out his sandwich-pack from under his jacket and offered it for the use of any who were hungry.

Fired by this youthful example, as well as by the preaching, others followed suit until eventually they were all handing their packed lunches to others and such a good meal was had by all that the disciples were left to clear up basket upon basket of litter.

This last is regarded by some people who are uneasy about miracles as a very satisfactory explanation, and for all I know it may be correct. But it is important to note that it does not really do away with the miracle at all; it merely moves it from one aspect of the situation to another. If the gospel story is accepted literally there is the miracle of the sheer production of large amounts of bread and fish out of nothing—a phenomenon amazing enough. Yet if the sandwich-pack version is accepted the miracle is transferred to the field of human relationships, and instead of the manufacture of bread and fish we have the creation in 5000 people of a desire to put the needs of others before their own. If I were to consider which was the greater phenomenon, the making of loaves and fishes or the sudden awakening of a genuinely unselfish attitude in 5000 Jews (or Englishmen, or Americans for that matter) I would have little doubt that the latter was an infinitely more impressive feat.

And this is really the crux of the matter. It is not very difficult to rationalise away the miraculous part of many of the incidents related in the gospels, but when all is said and done one is only brought up against some even more astounding act of power and transformation. A paralytic may perhaps have been suffering from some psychotic condition which inhibited the relay of motor responses to his muscles, and when Jesus told him to get up and walk he merely received the necessary psychological stimulus to free him from these limitations—but how much more miraculous it now seems if in just that brief exchange of glances and a few words the man could be given a release which throughout his life had been unobtainable. If the blind were merely spiritually blind, how astounding it is that the mere presence of Jesus could enable them to see themselves and their duties as they really were—and this in a society in which religious observance was the general rule.

I am not suggesting that this explanation of the restoration of sight to the blind is always satisfactory, for I do not think that it is. In one case at least there is a long account of how the hilarious patient was hauled before the authorities and asked to withdraw his statement that Jesus had cured him, and his parents were summoned to say whether or not he had in fact been cured. They confirmed the transformation, but being (like most people) frightened of courts and notoriety they refused to commit themselves as to the manner of the cure, although their son himself remained unshaken in his assertion.

The more one reads the gospel accounts of the healings and the nature miracles the more one notices the abundance of detail—the stern cushion of the fishing-boat, the way in which a paralysed man was let down from above because his friends could not get his stretcher to Jesus through the crowd, the remark that the body of Lazarus would be somewhat malodorous because he had been dead for several days. All these are the very things that an eye-witness would remember. They might of course be invented, but only by a remarkably talented story-teller, a man far more skilled in literature than a mere fisherman or inland revenue official or even a doctor could have been. A first-class novelist might well have added such touches, but the disciples and their adherents were not a branch of the PEN club, nor were they concerned to produce great literature. They were enthusiastic to tell people about their Lord, and they had no need to invent details of the house-keeping arrangements in Bethany. Nor, surely, would they have gone out of their way to report the association of Jesus with people of very dubious occupations if their purpose had been to build up a picture of a hero from sheer invention.

Quite apart from the detail the miracles themselves, whether they concern healing or such events as the stilling of a storm on an inland sea, are by no means told as things which one would expect but as events which amazed even the disciples themselves, used as they were to the power of their leader. There are continual references to the general astonishment—" What manner of man is this, that even the wind and the sea obey him?" That the happenings were regarded as being very much outside the run of normal experience is emphasised again and again. People were amazed, astonished, fearful, however much Jesus might insist (as he continually did) that it was the faith of a sick man which was the real key to his healing.

To me, both the circumstantial detail and the descriptions of the effects of miracles upon the bystanders make the stories ring astonishingly true; yet if the events themselves do not conform with the general current experience of the universe then some kind of explanation is still necessary— not so much in the way of analysis of the phenomena in terms of physics or chemistry, but to satisfy me that these things *could* have happened, if only because the central belief of the Christian is in the greatest miracle of all, not in the life of Christ but in his resurrection.

It is easy enough to give the answer that if the whole of the creation is within God, then clearly there was nothing at all remarkable about a storm being stilled if it was God's will. But this view is not altogether without difficulties, for if God's will is permanent (which a Christian must obviously believe to be the case) one may wonder why in our own day there are storms in many parts of the world which are *not* stilled, but overwhelm helpless and innocent people, and kill scores of thousands of sailors and fishermen every year. Why are these not stilled also—or for that matter, why are the conditions of the atmosphere so framed that hurricanes can happen at all? The answer to this is not one which it is possible to find if we think in terms of a God whose object is to feather-bed humanity as much as possible, a point which we can consider in more detail when we come to deal with the related problem of the general suffering of innocent and guilty alike. But the real stress of the gospel narrative of the storm on the lake seems to me to lie in the teaching of Jesus that in real human helplessness faith can save *physically* as well as spiritually. The universe as a mass of radiations, gravitational forces, and increasing entropy may seem at best indifferent to the fate of the individual and at worst actively menacing, but the assertion of the gospels is that this is a misconception, and that the world of the physicist is within the power and control of God. The cry of the individual in sheer helplessness and faith does not go unanswered— that is the teaching of Jesus as given in the storm scene, and it is left to the individual to test it for himself.

But if this is so, what of the million men blown to pieces at Verdun or Monte Cassino, of whom many thousands must have been sincere Christians? Could they not have cried " Save, Lord; we perish," and the mortar-shells would obligingly have altered their trajectories or simply failed to explode? Of course not, for the conditions are not in any way parallel. The danger on the battlefield is not one which is beyond human control. If shells are flying or atom bombs are burning up people by the hundreds of thousands, this is no case of human helplessness; the danger is only there because of the deliberate acts of nations and communities in which the Christian is involved quite as deeply as his fellows. If Christians could honestly say that throughout their lives they had striven with all their energy to destroy the causes of war and other evils, and to create what they call the " Kingdom of God on Earth," then the nine villages around Verdun of which not a single trace remains would, I suspect, still be there.

This does not necessarily mean that God is powerless to save from the hydrogen bomb and tank just because these things are human inventions. It is just that the case for intervention is not there. One can conceive that a time might come when humanity would be genuinely helpless in the face of its own works, but at the moment it can hardly be denied that if mankind genuinely wanted to be rid of these nightmare dangers it could dispose of them overnight. Not one of the millions killed during the gigantic battles of our modern wars would have been slaughtered if modern man had not been prepared to accept a way of life which included war as at least a possible activity, however distasteful. And for all we know some simple but faithful fisherman may indeed have been saved from a hurricane at the same moment that the genial inhabitants of London or Hamburg or Hiroshima were being crushed beneath the tottering buildings of their cities, and we have no reason to believe that many a faithful and innocent person—so far as humans can be innocent—may not have survived even those holocausts because of something which was not attributable just to chance, or to bad marksmanship on the part of enemy artillery or bomb-aimers.

I am not suggesting that the faithful escape and that the casualty lists are composed of the wicked. Everyone knows that this is not the case, and Jesus himself warned his hearers against assuming that the people who happened to be crushed by a collapsing tower were worse than those who escaped. But the Christian believes that nothing is beyond the power of God, and the miracle stories of the gospels roundly assert that God cares for the individual in need. They do not suggest, however, that it is his job to prevent mankind from stewing in the very unpleasant juice of its own deliberate making.

XI

HEALING AND MIRACLE

In discussing the nature of miracles I have used the word
"intervention," and this may suggest that God sits back to
watch the world go by with humanity wriggling in a complex net of mistakes, and that just now and again he shakes
himself and puts in a finger to turn off the wind or cure a
disease or whatever it may be. But such an idea is not
acceptable to the Christian with his assertion that God
sustains the whole universe. Perhaps it would be nearer
the truth to think of "Divine intervention" not as interference on the part of the deity but as a dropping of all the
barriers usually erected by man to exclude the somewhat
unwelcome recognition that the universe is not completely
random in nature. This is another way of saying that on
certain occasions individuals can become unusually aware
of the fact that the universe is not hostile or indifferent but
actually friendly. That it may have been so all along is not
altogether the point, for it is the awareness that counts.
And if this is the case—as I think it is—then awareness
of the power of God is an important element in every
event of a "miraculous" nature.

The writers of the New Testament referred to the events
which we call miracles by several terms, including "mighty
works" (or deeds of power) and "signs"—demonstrations,
one might say, either of the power of God or of the truth
of those things which Jesus was continually teaching.
Faith was what mattered, Jesus said; and any doubt was
dispelled by a forceful demonstration of the curing of a
disease which, medically speaking, would be thought in-
curable. It is worth noting that these mighty works were
not exclusive to Jesus as a kind of accessory of his nature:
in St. Luke's documentary record of the years after the
death of Christ there are many instances of precisely the

same kind of cure being wrought by the apostles. All sicknesses, even bacterial diseases, were regarded by Jesus as surmountable difficulties, the real nature of which was that they shut the individual off from a realisation of the transcendent power and love of God. If the patient sincerely believed that he could be cured, and that God really cared for him, that in itself opened the door for the healing power to flow in, and as far as the acts of healing are concerned it does not matter whether the faith was given by Jesus himself, or by his disciples in the first century A.D.—or by their successors in the twentieth century.

During recent years we have seen a reawakening of the realisation of this truth. Medical science from the renaissance to the twentieth century has made astonishing strides in developing all kinds of treatments from drugs to heart massage, and both preventive and curative techniques have reached such a pitch of skill and ingenuity that in little more than a hundred years the average length of life in Britain has actually been more than doubled. Until recently this ever-increasing success of medical research led people very naturally into thinking of human sickness in much the same mechanical terms that one would apply when dealing with a car which fired erratically or started badly in frosty weather, or suddenly stopped because of a blockage in a fuel pipe, and just as a careful motorist would take his car to a garage for a general tuning and checking every 5000 miles, so it became common for people to visit their doctors occasionally " for a quick check-over."

This outlook was no doubt very sensible in some ways, and it certainly helped research workers to make discoveries of the greatest importance, but it is now well recognised that a medical outlook which is framed entirely in terms of physical cause and physical effect is very far from adequate. Many cases do not fit happily into this pattern, and psychology, for all the dubious theories which may be found in some of its schools of thought, has done a great service in rediscovering the fact that the mind, whether conscious or subconscious, is far more intimately linked with the body than is a driver with his motor-car. Every doctor knows nowadays that a condition which appears to be entirely physical may have a deeper cause in some disquiet of the mind or spirit. Stomach ulcers and asthma are only two of the common complaints which are known to be frequently no more than a symptom of troubles of quite a different kind, and there are cases of actual paralysis of limbs for which no cause can be found in nervous lesions, and which yield to nothing more than the restoration by a doctor or psychiatrist of the patient's peace of mind, or his faith. In all these cases there must still be a *cause* of sickness, but it may be of quite a different nature from what might be suspected on a purely mechanical basis which leaves the whole realm of the mind and emotions on one side as irrelevant. Any family physician will know that the sheer fact of feeling utterly unwanted and unloved by all others can produce a whole range of symptoms which appear identical with those which can be caused by infections or endocrine disorders. This is really no more than a rediscovery of part of what the gospels allege—that faith (both in the sense of trust, or of what one believes) is a vital component of health.

To a certain extent this has never been entirely lost sight of. The Protestant churches have an instinctive dislike of the claims made for the bones of medieval saints as agencies for curing diseases, and they do not take kindly to the notion of praying to a saint as though he were a Harley Street specialist. It all smacks too much of witchcraft. Yet if he is honest even the most free-churchy free-churchman has to admit that these things sometimes work. Hundreds of thousands of people go to Lourdes, and I myself have watched from the deck of my own little boat in a French harbour the pathetic spectacle of the priests and nursing sisters carrying down the gangways of the S.S. *Canterbury* the endless stream of stretchers, and helping the cripples as they struggle on their crutches towards their special trains. That most of these will trail home again a week later in just the same condition not even the most fanatical believer in such pilgimages could deny, but the fact remains that every now and again a patient is completely cured. Not many perhaps, but one here and one there; and there can be little doubt that if they had not undertaken the trip they would not have been cured at all. This is not to say that they *could* not have been cured elsewhere; indeed, the non-Catholic may find it difficult to believe that Lourdes itself either as a locality or an institution has anything essentially curative about it. I suspect that this is perfectly true and that any place in the world could have been just as effective; but if Lourdes produces a cure when Buxton or Colorado Springs does not, then the scientifically minded Christian will inevitably be interested to analyse the reason.

As a hypothesis one may suggest that those who are cured at Lourdes, and whose cure is in essence miraculous (in the sense that no technical therapy is provided, and the transformation is against all purely medical probability) are those persons who are utterly convinced from the outset not only that they can be cured but that they will be. This hypothesis would certainly fit the fact that although cures occur they are comparatively rare in proportion to the huge flocks of the sick and crippled which make their way to the town. A visit to Lourdes is usually something of a last desperate gamble, and there must really be very few who can cross to France without a shadow of a doubt in their minds when they know that doctors and nurses and hospitals and orthopaedic clinics have already done their utmost but have been quite unable to help them. Lourdes, for all the assurances of the priest, is almost inevitably seen as a somewhat dubious proposition, and the suggestion that he should go there must seem to many a patient to be nothing more than a tactful way of saying that medically speaking the battle is lost and the case hopeless. To have real faith and confidence in the outcome of the journey must be exceedingly difficult, but just occasionally a person has this unquestioning conviction that God can cure them and that he will. The journey to Lourdes is undertaken in complete faith—and it works. The thought that the same assurance might have wrought the cure at the Elephant and Castle or in the Bronx or the Quartier

Latin does not cross the mind of the rare patient who goes to Lourdes and is healed; for had it done so he would have stayed at home and the same faith would surely have cured him—as no doubt sometimes happens if our hypothesis is correct.

We must now consider whether faith of a lesser kind can be curative; and if so, what is the difference (if any) in the effect. That relics, so abominated by the Protestant, are capable of some effect one cannot reasonably doubt—the records are far too numerous and well documented for them to be dismissed entirely as monkish fakes. Fraud there may often have been, and no doubt unscrupulous priests have often persuaded pilgrims to part with silver and gold to no purpose at all, but the faith of the patient has sometimes triumphed in spite of it all. And it is particularly interesting that cures should have been reliably reported (so far as one can accept any such reports at all) in cases where there can be no doubt that the relics were bogus, or where the gilded sarcophagus of some medieval saint was later opened and found to be empty! Yet this need not really surprise us at all, for on the hypothesis that it is the conviction or faith which induces the curative effect it clearly would not matter that the incidental trappings were bogus. The effect is surely not due to the authenticity of the bones or the bits of cross or whatever it may be. Provided a patient really believes the remains to be those of a " saint " and is convinced that because of some special and merited nearness to God that saint can present the prayer to God, and that God in his mercy will help in human helplessness, then the fact that the bones are those of a pig and that the saint is purely legendary does not influence the result. And why should it? The lesson of the gospel is that faith can bring the cure, not that bones work wonders.

It is of course only Roman Catholics who regard saints as intermediaries, but this is no accident. Before the Reformation we were, so to speak, all Catholics, and there is no doubt that an exaggerated regard for the saints not just for their example but for themselves led to a considerable degree of idolatry from which the Reformation was a very healthy reaction. Protestants in general and free-churchmen in particular have ever since reacted very strongly against any odour of idolatry—even when the smell has been something of an illusion—and above all they have rejected the idea that the individual has no access to God except through the priest or by way of the saints. Many free-churchmen will not let the word " saint " pass their lips even when referring to the disciples or to Paul the Apostle. They do not recognise this *corps d'élite* among Christians of the past, and they regard the very idea of praying through the mediation of a saint as sheer idolatry.

Yet the Roman Catholic who prays to a saint is not necessarily an idolater at all; there is a genuine element of humility in his concept that these special people were like himself in being human, but because of their courageous witness and their noble works they have, as it were, a particular and permanent nearness to God, and are in a position not entirely unlike that of private secretaries and executives to a prime minister or president. In connection with their own trade or their private affairs few people who needed government help or special legislation would be arrogant enough to badger the head of the state directly, but they might well lobby their constitutional representa-tive (who corresponds in this case to a " patron saint ") or try to have a word with an individual in influential circles. Such a one would not be so remote that he could not be expected at least to listen and perhaps to sympathise, and if convinced of the justice of a cause he could whisper a word in the ear of his chief from his own position of merited and respected responsibility. Recourse to a saint may seem to the Protestant a reflection of polytheism, but in reality it may reflect nothing more than reverence and humility.

The free-churchman on the other hand declaims roundly that all men are equal in the sight of God, implying that he himself is as good as the Pope or an archbishop, or even a saint (a category which he firmly refuses to admit even as far as to regard the St. as a courtesy title well earned for meritorious service—like a Légion d'Honneur or a knighthood in human affairs). This may be very true, but it can also lead to a kind of arrogance in approaching God which can as surely reach to sheer impudence as the Catholic view can to idolatry.

A person who invokes the aid of a saint in trouble or sickness may be so full of faith in God and yet so humble and so conscious of his own shortcomings that he feels that it would be presumptuous to ask God directly. Yet the faith of the relic-seeker may not always be of this order. It may consist in no more than a superstitious assurance that the relic will ring the bell. Such a belief is not centred upon Christ or any recognisable aspect of deity at all, but it must be admitted that this does not mean that it is utterly barren. Mere confidence in the skill of a doctor can work great transformations without the patient even pausing to consider whether the doctor has his skill from some divine source or not; and it seems at least likely that some of those cured by relics must have believed nothing more than that the relics would be effective, and if they regarded them as " holy " this was just a synonym for " magical."

Again, many pilgrims must have believed that the curative property was a direct attribute of some particular saint who, because of his special merit, was authorised to heal, almost as though he were on some supernatural Medical Register. This does not necessarily involve any Christian belief either, and it is interesting to note that it is the saint and not God who then receives the thanks—even in the personal column of *The Times,* where thanks to St. Jude are not infrequently given by people who are presumably sincere, although it is not quite obvious whether or not they expect St. Jude to read *The Times.* Very similar are the cures which are known from primitive and pagan religions too, and from no religion at all. From sheer conviction even the opposite of a cure can be induced, and if an African tribesman can be so convinced of his impending death that he can lie down listlessly and slowly fade away, this is surely the same sort of thing in reverse, and just another demonstration of the mere effect of mind over body.

I think it would be a mistake, however, to place all these cures on the same level as the gospel miracles. They certainly involve faith of a kind, but it is sometimes really no more than an irrational conviction on the part of the patient that he will get well; and if he recovers, then his ailment must be of the kind which can be cured (as many illnesses can) by sheer confidence. But in the miracle stories of the gospels we have something more than mere repeated demonstrations of the power of the mind on the body. Jesus did not ask the patients whether they were sure that they would get well; he certainly sometimes asked them if they really believed that *he* could cure them, but, on the other hand, he frequently took the faith for granted because of the way in which the sick presented themselves to him, and then he *commanded* the illness to be gone. And it was not the sufferers from anxiety neuroses who were brought to Jesus, so that they could be put right with a bland assurance that self-confidence and determination would set them up again; it was, according to the gospels (which relate the events with the greatest amazement), the lame, the injured and crippled, the blind and deaf, and the lepers—sufferers from handicaps of a highly physical nature upon which a mere trust that the condition would improve would have had little or no effect.

To Jesus, healing was inseparable from the nature of God. His instruction to the healed was that they should " glorify God," and often enough he preceded the cure with the somewhat surprising assertion, " Your sins are forgiven." This might be reasonable enough in, for example, a case of venereal disease where there was some direct connection between the medical condition and a wrong attitude to other people, and it is true that in general the Jews looked upon any illness as retribution. But Jesus quite clearly did not do so; his attitude was that realisation of the forgiveness of God, and of the care of God for the individual, brought a release of power which would overcome any obstacle however formidable, whether the depression was due to prolonged sickness, or the disadvantages of sheer poverty, or a genuine physical crippling. The faith involved was of a vastly different order from the mere trust in a doctor or hope in a magical cure, and it was this faith which was essential to the real healing, not only then but in our own generation too.

One should not have a picture of God who sits upstairs, counting units of the faith of an individual as a physicist might clock radioactivity with a Geiger counter, and then decides that old Mrs. Jones of Seven Dials has reached the threshold intensity and may be relieved of her rheumatoid arthritis as a reward for her endeavours. Healing is not a prize any more than sickness is necessarily a punishment, but the recovery of health may be a function (mathematically speaking) of the real awareness of the power of God and his care for the individual. It is extremely difficult for any sick person who has even a reasonable acquaintance with physiological processes and bacterial infections to place *complete* reliance on something so very different, and it may well be that this is why they are not cured more often.

But the suggestion that " mighty acts " of healing are not confined to the first century A.D. does not rely only on an acceptance of Catholic records. It is an experience of the everyday life of Christian missionary doctors of very different theological outlook. A surgeon in Africa may be out on his rounds in the bush when he encounters a case which he can diagnose as immediately fatal unless the condition can be dealt with at once. But the necessary treatment involves highly specialised apparatus which is not available within a thousand miles, and the patient is too ill to move. The proper drugs are not there either because rising costs and the concentration of the supporting churches back at home upon niceties of architecture or church order have deprived him of the possibility of having an all-inclusive stock at hand. He knows, however, that faith can heal, and that in this instance nothing else can. It is not enough for him just to think that faith might work; he has to be utterly sure that it will, and be able to convey the same complete certainty to the patient. Humanly speaking, both patient and doctor are utterly helpless and must put their entire faith in God's care for the individual. Just as in the gospels, it is a case of faith overcoming human helplessness and sweeping aside the barriers between the individual and the wholeness for which he longs. The healing which ensues may be rather in the nature of power to overlook or ignore the pain and the disease which is its origin, or it may be a transformation of a more physical kind, but healing it certainly is.

Healing through faith is now so thoroughly attested that certain men hold services and sessions of spiritual healing. Admirable though this may seem at first glance it is not necessarily so, for the danger of slipping over into a kind of witchcraft is very real indeed. Spiritual healing is not an alternative to the public health services or to the use of medical knowledge, and if it is so regarded by either its advocates or the patients this amounts to little more than medieval sorcery in theory, and nothing more than quackery in practice. The essence of healing of a spiritual kind is that it implies faith under conditions of helplessness, and the person who takes the view that it is cheaper to try the church than to pay a specialist's fee is by no means in such a condition. Moreover, the use of " means of grace " instead of medical techniques where they are available implies a fundamental misconception of medical achievements. It may well be that a priest or minister who helps a sick person to health is acting as an agent for a health which is of God in its origin, but we have no warrant for believing that doctors and nurses, and the men such as Pasteur and Jenner who were responsible for the great discoveries of medicine were any the less the agents of that same healing purpose.

If, as I have suggested, the Christian may regard the whole creation as being within God rather than as external to him, then knowledge of the workings of physiology is in essence a revelation of the divine. This may sound strange, but I think it may well be the truth, and it would indicate that man has a responsibility to use knowledge where it exists rather than to expect God to operate on his own. This is realised very fully by the missionary doctor, who does not go on his rounds as a species of Christian magician. He uses the great mass of medical learning and skill which has been developed over the centuries, and he does so as a Christian who believes that suffering and sickness set up barriers between man and God; he may very well have his patients continually in his prayers, but he does not go around laying his hands on malaria cases and invoking the assistance of God when the deity has already provided all the help that is necessary in the lives of those who traced the disease to its source and developed the drugs to deal with it.

Just the same is true of healings at Lourdes and elsewhere, and it may give us a clue as to why cures were much more commonly reported in earlier centuries. It is easy to suggest that lepers *thought* they were cured (though how a leper could ever think so if he was not it is rather hard to understand), but it may be more reasonable to accept that lepers were once utterly helpless and that their only relief lay in a tremendous act of faith. They may still be able to have the same faith, but to go on a pilgrimage would be a denial of the truth which has come through the patient researches on Hansen's bacillus.

XII

EVIDENCE OF RESURRECTION

I have suggested that the essence of the gospel miracles is that they are for the most part truly reported instances of the way in which faith could bring help in human help-lessness. But there is another element too, and that is the awareness of people that the help was there and was available through the power of God, whether mediated by Christ, or Peter, or some other disciple. And if we think of miracles in terms of faith *and awareness* rather than as monkey-business or conjuring tricks it at once becomes natural that they are not confined to the first century A.D. but are still with us to-day. Miracles of healing may be less frequently reported—though if one includes healing through the application of revealed truths of medicine and physiology they must be a million times as common as in the time of Christ—but sickness is only one among the difficulties before which an individual may be genuinely helpless. Death is another somewhat obvious one, and so are the storms and tempests of land and sea. The difficulties which may beset the individual from the wild forces of nature are parallel to those of disease in that they are not to be exorcised by a kind of spiritual meteorology when other methods are at hand. Just as the sick man should take the benefit of the medical knowledge available, so the boating enthusiast has no business to sail out into the Atlantic storms in some ill-found dinghy in face of all nautical knowledge and weather forecasts and then turn to incantations when he is being pooped, nor has the fool-hardy mountaineer any justification in imploring God to stop the avalanche when his fate could have been averted merely by refraining from climbing in the season when avalanches can confidently be expected.

There are still more varieties of human helplessness concerned with decisions as to right action in the intricacy of human relationships. It is here, more than anywhere else, that genuine bewilderment can overtake even the most devoted and conscientious person, and it is here, too, that miracles are commonplace. Outsiders may not call them miracles, but that does not matter. It is the experience of Christians famous or unknown throughout the centuries that one may suddenly be aware that a solution is given when there is complete helplessness and humble faith, and those are the conditions for a miracle to-day just as they were two thousand years ago.

A miracle is not a celestial conjuring trick, but a demonstration of the permanent reliability of God (which includes the whole arrangement of the universe) to aid the individual, accompanied by an awareness that this is the case. Some people are so thoroughly aware of this that nothing surprises them; others are so impervious to the awareness that they are never surprised—just because the occasion goes unnoticed. But I suspect that most of us are in between these two conditions and can sometimes be aware of (and surprised by) the fact that helplessness is relieved. And it is worth noting that certain particular characteristics are attached to many of these occasions, and in particular that the solution to a problem is often delightfully simple— so simple that the person involved had not even thought of it—and that the help is mediated through other individuals. That people in apparently insoluble difficulties just happen to bump into others who have some highly expert knowledge which provides the solution may seem to be chance, even if mathematically speaking the actual probability is negligible; but when they both feel that the occasion is one in which they can sense the liberating power of God at work (a strange and very recognisable feeling to those who have experienced it) there is no reason to doubt them. Not that it would matter if we did, for the experience of past ages seems to indicate that miracles do not wait on the approval of third parties. The Pharisees in the gospels were not at all pleased about the healings of Christ, but that did not prevent their happening.

Yet however reasonable miracles may be, we still have to recognise that this does not explain the mechanics of the nature miracles of the gospels such as the walking on the water; and if these are as correctly reported as they seem to be, then I can only see two ways in which one might regard them. One could perhaps imagine that what appears to be against the ordinary workings of nature only seems to be so because of our limited knowledge—just as television would have appeared as magic to our forefathers who knew nothing of cathode-ray tubes. This would imply that if we had a greater knowledge of the structure and order of the world around us, walking on the water would be no miracle at all. Alternatively one might think that the sheer uniqueness of the incarnation meant that the laws of nature, which are drawn from repeated and widespread phenomena, would not be relevant—which is another way of saying that all things were possible to Christ, however surprising they may be, and that as nothing could be more surprising than the personal appearance of God as a man in human history one would be somewhat simpleminded to expect the event to conform in every way to the local by-laws of atmosphere and water which were really within the being of which the person of Christ was the visible indication. Both these lines of thought seem to me reasonable, but there can be no telling which, if either, is correct. Essentially the miracle stories are a challenge, not to credulity but to faith.

Quite apart from trying to get to grips with the miracles related in the gospels and elsewhere, a Christian in this scientific age, as in all others, has to face up to the resurrection of Christ. This does not mean that he has to be able to give a foolproof account in terms of biochemistry or radioactivity or even parapsychology of what happened on that particular occasion, but he must accept that the resurrection is more than a myth. The theory of " Christ crucified " is not particularly difficult, if only because lawbreakers and political idealists are being hanged or shot in many countries of the world to-day, but the crucifixion is not the only plank of Christian faith. It may have been shocking, if not totally unexpected, that officialdom aided by the mob should hound a wise teacher to death, and no Christian would dismiss the crucifixion as a thing that did not matter. But Christianity is also founded quite uncompromisingly on that article of the creed " *He rose again the third day.*"

This assertion must inevitably strike the person who lives in a scientific age as quite a considerable camel to swallow. Even if Jesus was God concealed for the time being in the form of a pious country joiner, the crucifixion and entombment finished that particular episode for ever, one might think, though of course he might " live again " in the sense that Shakespeare is immortal 'or Karl Marx is not confined to his grave in Highgate Cemetery but still stalks the world. But immortality of this kind is something quite different from what Christianity alleges in the case of Christ. It is not claimed merely that Christ himself, and his verses and sermons, were unforgettable—haunting the mind like a political theory or the lines of Hamlet's soliloquy and inspiring people to a high-minded life. On the contrary, it is roundly asserted in the New Testament that Jesus himself actually left his tomb in a visible if perhaps rather changed form—it was a little while before people recognised him when they met him—and that he walked and talked for a matter of weeks before the " ascension " into a less tangible but equally real form. The Christian means two things when he talks about " the risen Lord "; he means not only the Christ with whom he can converse as clearly as he can with an acquaintance on the other end of a telephone line, but the actual Christ who emerged from the tomb and appeared to people who had been his friends and also (according to Paul) to others who had not. Without either of these basic beliefs Christianity would not exist as anything more than a pious respect for the teachings of a Jewish Confucius. If it were admitted that the death on the cross was the end, then Christianity would be no more than worship of a dead hero. But this does not mean that the story was necessarily invented. Genes are necessary to those who forecast in applied genetics, but this is no proof that they are sheer inventions either. The evidence for genes is extremely good, and so must the evidence for the resurrection have been if men could get away with such an inherently improbable story. For right from the start the assertions of the Christian Church about the resurrection flew in the face of all normal human experience. The sheer unlikeliness of such a thing is nothing new, and it does not stem from our superior knowledge of bacterial decomposition and internal decay.

This, I think, is often overlooked. From our position of modern technology we so easily tend to look back on other ages and think of former generations as composed of rather gullible people who would believe anything, but if we really think that it is our scientific knowledge which raises question marks in our minds about the resurrection this implies that we credit the citizens of first-century Jerusalem with absolute imbecility. It really suggests that one afternoon a member of the city council walking down the street might have met a friend, and a conversation could have ensued as follows :—

"Good afternoon, Joseph. Anything interesting happen down your way lately?"

"I don't think so, Nathaniel. A dead man got up and walked out of his tomb after a couple of days, but that's about all. Nothing worth mentioning ever seems to happen these days."

"No, it doesn't. Well, I must be on my way, and I'll see you at the council meeting."

It would be crediting the Jews with incredible *naïveté* to assume that they could accept the resurrection just because they had not taken chemistry and biology at preliminary level. Besides, a glance at the gospels and at the first few chapters of the sequel written by Luke shows that the allegation that Jesus had risen caused the greatest stir. The account of the resurrection in the gospels and its preaching by the apostles was never even remotely within the bounds of everyday human experience.

There are only three possibilities. Either the whole tale (including the details about local astonishment) is a fiction;

or the details of the impact of the story on the Jews are true
enough but the actual resurrection was a deception im-
provised by the disciples after the crucifixion, because they
realised that a dead Jesus could hardly be thought an
incarnation of God; or the resurrection did indeed happen,
much as outlined in the accounts.

As regards the first, it hardly seems likely that one could
invent a situation which involved startling allegations about
the local authorities and maintain that it had all happened
a comparatively short while before and certainly during
the lifetime of many of those to whom one was spinning
the yarn. Paul, too, was continually writing open letters
about the resurrection, and there is no record of people
resident in the area having attempted to deny what he
related. Some of the Athenians were somewhat taken aback
by his assertions in an address, but so far as we know they
made no attempt to refute him on the facts. Within decades
of the death of Jesus men and women of many nationalities
were letting themselves be torn in pieces rather than deny
not just the life and teaching of Jesus *but the resurrection*;
some were simple people, not easily brought to face death
for a myth of no relevance, and others (like Paul) had
highly trained minds which had made them instinctively
reject the possibility of resurrection until they had actually
encountered the risen Christ in person. It is beyond belief
that all this could be based on a conspiracy. Besides, if one
had wanted to fabricate a story around the person of Jesus,
nothing could have been less likely to deceive than such a
vastly improbable tale as that he came to life two days after
being crucified.

This also applies to the second possibility, namely that
the narrative of events is true except that the followers of
Jesus thought up the actual resurrection stories right away
in order to establish some special status for their master.
If this could have happened it does not reflect much credit
on the city council and the Roman administration, for
nothing could have been a more damaging slander upon
them and yet it could easily have been cut down to the
roots by the simple expedient of producing the dead body.

But far from even suggesting anything so obvious they allowed the city to reach a seething state of turmoil, and their only reaction was to threaten people with a beating if they did not keep quiet about what had happened. These threats, and even the stoning to death of Stephen, apparently made no difference at all. "With great power gave the apostles witness of the resurrection of the Lord Jesus" —and though the priests had only to produce the corpse in order to discredit them as complete charlatans they were unable to do so. Anyone viewing the course of events as analytically as possible is bound, I think, to conclude that there can only have been one reason for this failure : the body was not there. Had it perhaps been stolen? According to St. Matthew this very handy explanation was the first thing that came to the minds of the council, and they even paid the guards to say so, but it was not enough to convince people—presumably because there were too many independent witnesses whose story was very different.

So it seems that neither of the fraud theories can really be maintained, and as we are then left only with the highly improbable notion that the resurrection actually happened very much as related, we have to look at the evidence. Firstly there are the New Testament assertions about eyewitnesses numbering, we are told, as many as five hundred on one single occasion, to say nothing of numerous appearances of the risen Christ to smaller numbers on several other occasions. Even if one could really believe all these stories to be invention one is still left with the very remarkable fact that personal knowledge of the risen Christ, not just as an ideal but as something very real and concrete, has been alleged by many others not only in the first century A.D. but in every succeeding age. There has been nothing to be gained by those who have made these assertions, but on the contrary their refusal to retract them has often enough led to torture and death. Just as in the days of the apostles, threats have almost always proved powerless to induce a denial.

Most impressive of all, however, is the transformation wrought by the event upon the small group of disciples.

Artisans and illiterate fishermen, a tax-man and one or two lower middle-class Jews of no particular ability, their hopes were utterly dashed by the trial and hanging of their leader. We do not need to doubt the truth of the gospels when they tell us how the little band was easily scattered and how even Peter, the bluff fisherman who alone was ready to oppose the temple guard with an unskilled slash with a sword, was so broken that he dared no longer admit that he was an associate of Jesus. Cowed and humiliated, the handful of men and women dispersed whilst the city crowd deliriously cheered the decision to put Jesus on the cross. How then can one explain the astonishing behaviour of these same men a few weeks later, if nothing of an exceptional nature had happened in the meantime?

The New Testament makes excellent reading on this point. Quite undramatically, Luke the physician relates how these same untutored men were shortly to be found addressing massed meetings and walking into the temple to tell the assembled crowds that their own religious leaders had murdered God. No wonder the temple authorities were " grieved " ! A parallel in our own day would be that a couple of trawlermen who had been bound over to keep the peace should walk up the steps of St. Paul's, wave the good dean and the canons to one side, and proceed to tell them in the bluntest language that their theology was nonsense and that the clergy themselves were guilty of hideous crimes, adding that they happened to know this because a former friend of theirs who had come on their boat had told them so. Even in this tolerant age the worthy dean might be upset; but however he felt about it personally it is not very likely that what the trawlermen said would rock the whole system of established religion to its foundations.

Look forward a year or two, and these same men and their associates (who now include at least one brilliant theologian) were touring almost the whole of the known world, causing riots and disturbances on an unprecedented scale and openly defying the armed might of the Roman Empire which held rule throughout the area with a grasp as absolute as the modern control of Soviet Russia over the lands beyond the Iron Curtain. Not that we even need the narrative of Luke's record to tell us this, for the reverberations of what these simple men had experienced were soon shaking the empire, and the doctrine of the resurrection was in Rome itself—even in the Imperial Court. It swept over the map of Europe, crossed the Channel to Britain and grew in strength until again one or two men could sell it with their lives among such tough communities as the Franks and the Frieslanders and the Vikings. This is no story of ancient and dubious documents but the sheer fabric of the history in which we live. Christianity, with its fantastic claim about the resurrection, has been powered to sweep into every corner of the world in the face of tremendous odds. Whatever else may be said about the history of the early Church it is at least clear that what happened immediately after the death of Christ must have been something very remarkable indeed if it could provide an impetus so irresistible and could endow those who knew about it with such courage and determination, when a few weeks earlier they were laughable failures in the eyes of the whole community.

I do not see how any person who surveys the course of history can doubt that some overwhelming event took place at that time, and as no alternative to the resurrection was offered by way of explanation in the early centuries of our era or has been put forward ever since, then even to the non-Christian the circumstantial evidence must, I think, be seen as very much in favour. If on top of this the " risen Lord " has been declared down the ages to be the personal experience of people in hundreds and thousands, then either this is confirmatory or they have all been deluded. And when we consider that assertions of this kind have come from highly practical men such as generals and scientists, from very unemotional men such as seamen and farmers, and from the highly trained critical minds of classical scholars too, the theory of general delusion is rather difficult to sustain. Nor does it matter in the least if in a number of primitive cultures some legend of a dying and revivified fertility god should also be found. The fact that pornographic novels and Shakespeare's plays are both available in book form does not mean that Shakespeare was nothing but a pornographer.

It is not easy, on the evidence, to escape acknowledging that what Christians call the "resurrection" is an item of history. Yet the fact remains that such an event is quite outside the run of our normal experience. People die, their bodies decay, and bacteria and invertebrates dispose of them. What could have happened at the resurrection if this was not the pattern?

To this question I can no more give the certain answer than can anyone else, but there are several lines of thought which a scientific Christian might put forward. For instance, if matter is no more than an arrangement of energy then it is perfectly conceivable (if surprising) that where the sheer essence of the whole creation was poured into human form, the body could dissociate into sheer energy and re-distil as it were, outside the tomb, in a state which was on the average more energy than matter but definitely material enough to have some shape and substance. Some people think of the resurrection in this way, and they can point out that the gospels give a wealth of detail which somewhat suggests transformation of an electrical nature; the meteorologic effects and the radiating appearance described in St. Matthew, the frightening effect upon the women of St. Mark, the semi-material descriptions in St. Luke, all fit the theory. Others would simply say that to them the resurrection means a complete restoration of the physical body of Christ, and that it was perfectly natural for God to be immune to the death which otherwise afflicts the creation—though this, I think, implies that the death on the cross was not a real death at all. Yet others would think in terms of a revivification of a normal but formerly dead body, and cite Lazarus as an indication that this might be so. For all I know they are right, though personally I do not think that the New Testament appearances of the risen Christ confirm their view. Others would attribute these descriptions to imagination, in the sense that what people were aware of was the mysterious presence of the personality of Jesus which they had to describe in the best terms they could muster. Others again may maintain that the resurrection story is really a parable to illustrate an eternal truth of a purely spiritual kind—that the body of Christ could be killed but his real essence was invulnerable. This, they would say, is a lesson to us on the relationship between our own personalities and our physical bodies. There may be much truth in this, but it is a theory which cannot be held unless one considers much of the gospel detail of the resurrection to be invention; nor is it clear why this spiritual immortality alone (which Jesus had preached all along) should suddenly have had so dramatic an effect on his followers.

Finally one can even believe that the *apprehension* of the resurrection is a mystical appreciation of the essential truth that the power and designs of man are of no avail whatsoever when set against the power and purpose of God of which the physical universe is a reflection. This, too, may be very true in its way, but it falls short of explaining what happened in the history of the early Church.

The truth is that we do not know the intimate processes of the event, and although science may one day make it more comprehensible it seems unlikely that we shall ever understand the resurrection in the sense that we could say just how it worked. The details we have are tantalisingly sketchy, and however much we may regret that physicists with Geiger counters and infra-red cameras were not on the spot at the time, the fact remains that they were not. And on the whole I think that this is as it should be, for Christianity is not an equation of physics. It involves faith, an invitation to take a plunge of belief and see whether one's individual experience then confirms it. To want to know just *how* the resurrection occurred and the precise form it may have taken is a natural longing of the human mind both now and in earlier ages. Some would go further, and say that it is an insidious temptation to which the mind of man has always been subject, and that it should be resisted because it diverts attention from the sheer fact to irrelevant detail. Perhaps they are right, but I am not so sure that a longing for practical understanding is necessarily wrong.

Nevertheless it may well be that if the information were to be had there would be no challenge on which to stake one's shirt and one's life. " Christ is risen " has proved the most powerful message the world has ever known, but it has always involved more than the acceptance of an intellectual proposition, and if the event had been capable of reduction entirely to terms of physiological detail it might have been no more inspiring than " Queen Anne is dead " —an assertion which needs no faith for its acceptance, but a mere turning up of the dusty state records for August 1714.

But one thing is certainly clear. Beside the resurrection, whatever its physical nature may have been and however one may interpret it, the other miracles of the gospels are slight (though not insignificant). And if, as I have suggested, the real nature of a miracle is that the event is accompanied by exceptional awareness of the limitless power that can come to the aid of human helplessness, this would be an essential component of the resurrection too. The teaching of the apostles was very clear on this point. Acceptance of the risen Christ brought a quite startling apprehension of the fact that evil in any shape or form and even death itself could be overcome by the power of God. And that was why the teaching of the resurrection swept across land and sea with a vitality which has never been equalled.

XIII

PAIN IN THE CREATION

We are not yet at the end of what a Christian must include among the planks on which his central claim is supported. He must accept that the creation is in some way within God's care and activity, and he must recognise that the gap between the perfection of God and the perfection of which man is capable was bridged in the person of the historical Christ. If I do not express this point in more detail it is perhaps because many, including the gospel writers, have already done so more ably, and also because the precise interpretation of the incarnation varies somewhat from one branch of the Church to another. But *all* Christians are agreed about the event itself, and they are equally agreed that there was more than just life and death and resurrection in the appearance of Christ in human history. That Christ quite voluntarily allowed himself to follow a course of action which inevitably led to the cross, and that by so doing he took upon himself the sin of all men in every generation, and thus " redeemed " them to a state in which reconciliation with God was possible—that is the Christian faith, and it involves more than acceptance of the mere life and teaching and resurrection of Jesus himself. The key-word here is *sin*. Without acceptance of the idea that sin is a very genuine thing, then the rest of the statement is meaningless. Whether we like it or not, Christianity involves a square belief in sin.

Now what a Christian means by sin is not, as some people would have one believe, adultery or prostitution, or anything to do with sex at all. Of course sex may be involved in the sinful acts of some people, but although the term " living in sin " popularly means having (or being) a mistress we are all of us according to the Christian living in sin, whether we are pagans, or ordinary laymen like myself, or bishops. Some people have the idea that Christians hold a very good opinion of themselves, but this should be the opposite of the truth. The Christian church is a vast assemblage of people who are aware of *their own* sinful inclinations and deeds, and recognise their need of redemption. No member of a church can be complacent or self-satisfied in the least.

Sin means the deliberate choice of what is wrong. Not wrong according to the law perhaps, for adultery and prostitution are allowed under the law, though they are generally agreed to be wrong. To eject a tenant who has fallen on bad times and cannot pay the rent is something which a court might be expected to uphold as reasonable, but under most circumstances we may feel it to be a great wrong—whatever the judicature may decide. In thinking of these things as wrong we assume from the start that there is some higher standard than the law of the land against which actions can be judged, and the Christian thinks in terms of "good" and "evil." He could never accept the notion of sin except on the basic assumption that there really is such a thing as evil, and that there is some absolute and transcendent standard, a moral law. Sin is a deliberate offence against this moral law, and one cannot have sin unless this law exists any more than one could commit an income tax offence if there were no national fiscal laws and it was just left for everybody to pay what he liked to the state.

On the other hand one might have a tax law where there was no one there to pay the taxes, and in case this should seem unlikely one has only to consider Denmark. There are some 300 uninhabited islands within the provinces of the Danish crown, but the laws of the Danish treasury extend over them just the same. A tax *offence* could only exist there if these isles were lived on, but the absence of taxpayers and tax evaders does not make the regulations disappear in smoke.

It is very much the same with the moral law which the Christian believes to operate through the universe as a reflection of God's nature. The moral law, he maintains, extends over the Moon or Mars, as well as over the Earth, and it did so before there were any men to offend it, so there are really two quite distinct aspects of the problem of a moral law to be considered. There is the way in which man can apprehend the law and respond to it; and there is the operation of the same law quite apart from human action.

Many of the relationships within the universe are demonstrable, and one sometimes wonders whether the existence of this alleged moral law might be demonstrated too, or perhaps even disproved. I think the answer is that it cannot be shown to be either true or untrue by anything which we normally understand by scientific proof or checking through experiment, and this is partly because the law is not conceived of as a mere description of events. Scientific " laws " may be demonstrable, but they are altogether of another order, and even such precise and practical formulas as Boyle's law and Mendel's laws merely provide man-made and very useful categories to label and tag great numbers of experiences. We may well find that in every case investigated the volume of a gas at constant temperature is inversely proportional to the pressure, but Boyle's law is a human construction (the work, in fact, of the Hon. Robert Boyle). Boyle did not *arrange* that a gas would show this relationship; he only discovered the fact. The Christian notion of the moral law, however, is that God did indeed arrange it, and it is part of the essence.of his nature.

A Christian might perhaps think that Boyle's law reflects the ability to *demonstrate* experimentally a particular facet of one part of God's nature which is reflected in the physical existence of things in general (and in the constitution of gases in this particular instance), and that the moral law is another and perhaps far more vital aspect of God's nature which we should also be able to demonstrate experimentally. But this I think is a mistake, for there is a real difference between the two. The behaviour of gases happens whether we are there or not, but evil does not happen. It is *done* by men. If the world were devoid of

men equipped with some sort of freedom to choose what
they do themselves, then there would be no actual evil
unless evil were an inherent quality of the universe itself.

But might this not be precisely the same in the case of
good? If evil springs from human action, good might also
be inseparable from human deeds. It is obvious enough
that what we think is good can certainly be done by man,
but if we assume that good can *only* take shape through
human choice then the universe as such is neither good nor
bad, moral or immoral or a bit of both, but just amoral. It
is very tempting and highly convenient to think that this
is the case, and many people do so. But a Christian can
surely not subscribe to such a belief, for he asserts that the
creation is within God, purposeful, and *good*. He must
therefore regard the whole creation as essentially good,
and accept that evil is no more than an inherent possibility
which can become crystallised through human rebellion
against that same goodness with which the sheer fabric of
things is shot through.

This view is none other than that of "the fall," and I
think it corresponds very closely with such experience of
the universe as any individual can have, but it must nevertheless make the Christian stop and consider. If evil is not
present without man, and the universe is not amoral but
actually good, then what did Christ mean when he said
that not a sparrow fell to the ground without our heavenly
Father knowing it? Surely he did not mean that one more
dead sparrow was logged and that was that. He specifically taught that God loves the whole creation.

It is not just a matter of whether sparrows and other
creatures are expendable, but of the whole catalogue of
events in nature, and the relentless system of attack and
injury and extermination by which it appears to work.
Modern discoveries in biology, coupled with the theory of
evolution, stress the extraordinary ingenuity and specialisation of structure which enables one living creature to maim
or kill and devour another. Of course we are all of us
familiar with this in our everyday life, and even as I write
I can see out of my window a thrush pulling at a worm on

the lawn, dragging it from its hole to swallow it and digest it. Near by in the bushes a cat is lurking to pounce on the unwary thrush, and for all I know a dog is watching the cat for an opportunity to catch it off its guard and bite through its neck. Perhaps the dog has tape worms absorbing food from its intestines, and maybe its liver is riddled with other parasitic worms which before long will kill it. Or, for all I know, the dog is at this very moment picking up the germs of hard-pad and a week hence it will be dying. No aspect of this situation is due to the intervention of man; nature is "red in tooth and claw" and if I believe evil to be a function (mathematically speaking) of deliberate human choice, then I have to believe what I see taking place in the world of nature is not evil. It is either amoral or actually good. This is really no new problem, even if science has helped to throw it into sharper relief. The suffering and pain and death which are found from end to end of the catalogue of living creatures are inescapable, and Paul wrote of the whole creation groaning and labouring.

Easy though it may be to think of nature as amoral, the Christian's assertions about the nature of God oblige him to decide that in spite of appearances this system of struggle and pain and death among animals is genuinely good. At the same time there must be many who find it far from easy to convince themselves that this can be the case, and that a creation involving widespread suffering can possibly represent undiluted good or reflect the activity of a God whose essence is that of love. A possible and favourite solution is to try and exorcise the essential painfulness of life and assure oneself that it is really quite illusory. One may say, for instance, that when a cat plays with a mouse before finally eating it, the cat is not being cruel but just being a cat as evolved; yet although this may well be true, as I think it is, it still does not make it any more pleasant for the mouse to be eaten. And as to pain, one can suggest that animals do not genuinely feel pain or distress or even fear, but in certain situations they merely react with squawks and squeaks into which we read emotions of our own. But this I do not think one can honestly believe. The reaction of a teal when its mate has fallen to the shot of a sportsman, the scream of a rabbit when face to face with the bared teeth of a stoat, the whimpering of a dog whose paw has been crushed in the grip of a mole-trap—it is comforting to try to convince oneself that these are automatic reactions containing nothing more of pain or fear than the ringing of an alarm clock, but the attempt so far as I am concerned is not very successful. Defence mechanisms and escape reflexes may have been essential in the evolution of successful creatures, and pain undoubtedly serves as a warning and sets off a train of responses (as when one touches a hot sauce-pan handle and immediately pulls one's hand away), but that does not make it more pleasant to endure or equate it automatically with love. Besides, the pain of a creature racked by the torture of an open and gangrenous wound is not a warning of anything—except, perhaps, of approaching death.

There are some Christians who still believe in "special creation" in the sense that God created all living types comparatively recently and in a final condition, ready to get on with the business of living. Quite apart from the mass of scientific evidence to the contrary I think it is fair to ask how they can overcome this particular difficulty. If the living types which inhabit the world are all quite separate manufacturing lines of the creator then the picture they give us of that creator is not an attractive one and it certainly involves something very different from love. But to the Christian who faces up to the belief that the creation has been through evolution the situation is not so hopeless. He can see that these mechanisms of struggle and pain and suffering have always been absolutely inherent in the system of evolving life, which appears to be the only conceivable system which could have led from agglomerations of matter, across the border line into live organisations of molecules, and onwards and upwards through the rolling centuries and geological ages to the incredible organisation of matter in a form which is not only clever enough to make television cameras and space rockets but can love (and hate) and actually be conscious of God.

I think the debt of Christians to Darwin is immense, for he laid the foundations of a greater understanding of the way in which man and the animals have been formed, and provided the means of appreciating the relationship of the pain in nature to the love of God. It is commonplace for an individual to recognise that his own existence has involved the sheer physical pain, ungrudgingly borne, of his own mother in pregnancy and at his birth, and I think that the pain of the creation can perhaps be seen as something very closely related to it, for it was necessary to the whole emergent process of improvement and adaptation which has led from the primeval seas to life in a cottage or a suburban house. In the relentless inter-specific competition of animals, in the scream of the rabbit and the cry of fledgeling ducks as the black-headed gulls swoop to peck out their eyes and devour them, an extension of that same birth pain is there none the less. And without it I myself could not exist, and if I believe that Christ on the cross carried the sheer burden of the sin of man I can also believe that every living creature past and present carries the burden of my own life and freedom. God may well "know" when a sparrow-hawk dives and a sparrow is maimed or killed; but more important (if I can put it that way) is that I myself should realise that this is happening, and look upon nature not just in sympathy or sorrow, but in respect and love for the little creatures which are part of the single process which led out of chaos towards that awareness of God which is offered to me to accept or reject.

I can imagine that some would admit that this is not sheer romance and that a feeling of gratitude to creatures of the past would not be unreasonable; but they may still wonder why the suffering of nature could not be confined to what one might term the "main railway line" of evolution. Once the mammals had arisen the lines of reptiles and birds might have been discontinued, or at least allowed a gay and carefree and perhaps strictly vegetarian life.

But it seems to me that man could never have emerged unless creatures had not only had an infinite capacity for variation and an astounding resilience, but also an almost obstinate hold on life itself. The very same mechanism without which man was an impossibility has an indestructible capacity for evolving, adapting, and radiating into specialisation. One cannot take the living creation and decide that one creature is good and another either useless or pointless, a mere receptacle of unpleasant reflexes. It was Linnaeus and not God who classified creatures and laid down a system of taxonomy. To a biologist there may be hundreds of thousands of types of living creatures, each separate from all the others though occasionally closely linked to each other in interdependence; but I suspect that this attitude, though useful in the laboratory, is based on distinctions which are not in the true essence of life itself. It is very reasonable, and perhaps somewhat nearer the truth, to forget the distinctions of species and genera which the biologist has to use in his researches, and accept the whole of nature from virus to elephant and hook-worm to humming-bird as one single astounding and integrated reflection of the power and love of the creator, with its culmination in the awareness of man. And if this is so, then just as we must think of our fellow men as equals and brothers under the fatherhood of God, regardless of intellect or race or colour, so too we may not be very wide of the mark if we regard all living creatures not just as shareholders in the joint stock of life, but as simpler beings who may have no awareness of the purpose of it all, but whose suffering is essential to the awareness which is ours. In this sense the creation is good *even in its pain*.

If it is possible thus to look at nature and accept that the suffering is real and is an essential part of the goodness and love of God in the creation which has culminated in man, then this is not to say that the suffering of animals is something to which we should be indifferent. On the contrary, if the groaning of the past and present of the creation were through our own choice of evil to be rendered vain and ineffectual, then it would surely become an evil thing. It

is only because the pain of creation is absolutely pregnant
with the opportunity of bringing about a relationship of
love between man and God that it is good, and if we deny
this relationship or deliberately turn our backs on it, it is
not our own sin that becomes an offence against God,
but the whole of the pain of the lesser creatures is flung in
his face as well. I believe it may well be a realisation of
this which is at the bottom of the kindness and care towards
animals which has been so dear to many of the greatest
and most saintly Christians.

Our responsibility to the lesser creatures may thus be
far greater than we always realise, and a callousness towards
their suffering is perhaps one of the worst and most arrogant
offences of which man is capable. The pain of creation is
only redeemed by man's reconciliation to God, and suffering
needlessly inflicted by man on other creatures must surely
be beyond all excuse. I have said *needlessly* because it seems
clear enough that man is not outside the system itself, and
his sheer existence must involve his control of many
creatures, but there is all the difference between the destruction of plague-carrying rats or the slaughtering of beef
cattle or poultry, and the delight in killing and maiming
other creatures for a Saturday afternoon's entertainment.

XIV

SUFFERING AND GOOD

There are few people who go through life without sickness and occasional pain, and some individuals are obliged to carry a very heavy load of physical or mental suffering. One of the incidents recorded in the gospels tells of a woman who had had a haemorrhage for thirty years, and our modern hospitals and institutions contain great numbers of men and women who seem destined to lie there in helplessness or in pain, or in the stupor of pain-alleviating drugs, until their life ebbs finally away. One may well wonder what is the purpose of their lives, and how their condition can possibly conform with the notion that humans are all within the embracing fatherhood of a just God.

It was perhaps possible for our forefathers often to convince themselves that suffering was in some way the direct result of sin, or else was inflicted as a sentence of punishment by a God who acted as a celestial magistrate, and if the excruciating pain of certain diseases seemed a somewhat harsh punishment it could be pointed out that strict but virtuous parents sometimes beat their own children in order to correct and educate them, and that to give one's own child a thrashing was no indication of lack of love but rather the reverse. I myself have heard this explanation of suffering given from the pulpit, and though I do not doubt that it could conceivably contain a grain of truth I am quite sure that it cannot cover the many cases in which the most blameless people may suffer prolonged and fearful pain of either a physical or a mental kind.

Then it is sometimes said that suffering is sent as a challenge, a kind of test as to whether an individual will still keep his faith and not turn round and curse God. And it is pointed out that intense suffering does not always lead to moral collapse, but occasionally to a wonderful mellow-

ing of character and a love for others so strong that the
suffering itself seems to vanish. This may well be true,
but such answers do not satisfy everyone. The point is
that one must be able to equate the suffering of the *innocent*
with the existence of a loving God, and I think it is not
unreasonable to wonder whether a mere human parent
could conceivably use such techniques in bringing up his
children. Surely no father worthy of the name would give
his own children a hiding just to see if they could stand it,
or in the hopes that it might make them patient and wise
and kindly disposed towards other children. And if we
cannot believe this of human love, how can we believe it
of the love of God?

Of course the problem is not new, and the book of Job
is a useful reminder that the reason why the innocent and
devoted person should suffer as he sometimes does has
puzzled thinking people for more than two thousand years.
But I think that modern discoveries of the causation of
certain kinds of sickness have thrown the matter into sharp
relief. For example, a particular rearrangement of the
molecular structure at one precise point on one of the
chromosomes of the sex cells of a man or woman will have
no effect upon them or upon their immediate descendants,
but if it is doubled up by the marriage of a carrier with
another individual who, quite unknown to himself, is
carrying a chromosome with an identical allele or arrangement of genetic material, then there is a one-in-four chance
that a child will have the development of its nervous
system drastically affected. Such a child will be born in a
more or less normal condition, but the double dose of the
" infantile amaurotic idiocy " gene which it has received will
halt the further development of its brain and nervous
system, which will begin slowly to degenerate. A few years
later the child will be dead, and nothing whatsoever can
be done to avert its fate.

Now we cannot seriously imagine that the parents have
done anything to deserve this, or that their suffering as
they see their child wasting away in idiocy is necessarily a
healthy experience for them. In fact they have not been

selected at all to undergo the frustration of being the parents of such a child, for not only may the gene have run down their families for literally hundreds of years in a single and ineffective condition but its incidence in a double dose in this one particular child is sheer chance, and three children out of four will escape it. And as for the affected child itself, surely its utter innocence is as clear as the futility of its short human life. To say that such a child does not suffer is merely to play with words. It may not experience pain, but it is to forfeit its life before it has gone much further than infancy, and such life as it will have is devoid of understanding and of any real awareness of the world around it. The same is true of the mongoloid idiot; whether produced by a dominant gene or by some obscure endocrine exhaustion on the part of its mother it will live and die as little more than an inefficient animal. It is sometimes said that for all we know such children are fully aware of the love of God and of their parents, but we certainly do *not* know that they are—and if the apprehension of love or of truth demands any use of the mind at all then it seems, to say the least, rather improbable.

Perhaps part of our difficulty stems from clinging to the belief that suffering is inflicted. Men often inflict suffering and pain upon others, but we have no warrant to believe that God does so, and to think that he might is surely a denial of the very notion of loving fatherhood. Nor can we possibly believe that there is necessarily any connection between pain and sin. It may be attractive to the self-righteous to see something of the kind in the incidence of venereal disease leading to general paralysis of the insane, but plenty of white-slavers can be seen to escape this particular fate and live on the fat of the land.

If science has done anything to deal a final death blow to these notions of the cause of suffering (which are certainly not Christian ones) we can be thankful. And perhaps we can realise that pain and suffering in man are a part of that which runs right through nature, and that it is absolutely inherent in the mechanism of genes and physiology and evolution which makes our own existence possible. The true wonder is not that an idiot child should be born, but that any creature at all could arise equipped with the possibility of awareness of God and a will with which to respond.

It is at this point that we can turn from what science is revealing to us as a part of total truth and consider what the gospels have to say on the subject. As a layman I think there are three points which we must not fail to take, and the first of these is that Jesus sought wherever possible to rid men of pain because it so obsessed their thoughts and limited their lives that it deflected them from concentrating on their responsibility towards God. In trying to heal we are certainly acting in the highest tradition of Jesus himself. Secondly, and not conflicting with this, it seems clear that he did not regard pain itself as necessarily evil. It is impossible to imagine suffering more excruciating than that of a crucified man dying on a cross; indeed the Romans, who were experts in matters of this kind, very well knew what a frightful torture it was, with no release but the slow creeping of death over a body racked by the agony of the splintered bones crushed by the clubs of the guards—which was the procedure used for the thieves, though in the case of Christ an extra refinement was added by nailing through the hands and feet. This incredible burden of pain, to be borne not by some unsuffering demigod of fiction but by a man with a man's anatomy and physiology, was accepted by Christ without one single word of deprecation of the pain itself. Whatever else he did, he did not go to the cross to exorcise pain.

Finally, the teaching of Christ was that this life was in the nature of a preparation, and I think it is only within the acceptance of this that the pain and suffering of the innocent can be seen in their true light. The " life to come " is not a thing which can be proved from the existence of suffering, but at least one may realise that some of the most baffling contradictions about mankind begin to evaporate when human life is regarded within this context. By way of parallel we might imagine some strange flying-saucer pilot from elsewhere in the universe being shown round the infant ward of one of our maternity hospitals under the impression that children lived only to the age of three. He would note that the existence of the children seemed to consist very largely of bouts of crying, screaming, dirtying their nappies, cutting their milk teeth and sleeping, and he might well wonder that human parents could inflict on them a life containing so much unpleasantness for no return other than a certain amount of gurgling affection. If infants led such limited lives fraught with tears and pains, might it not have been better that their rather short and pointless existences had never been begun? Only when the news was tactfully broken to him that the struggles of infancy were merely the prelude to the years of adolescence and maturity with all that they could bring in the way of work and love and devotion and gaiety would he realise that the state of infancy was perhaps not so cruel and pointless as he had imagined.

This, I think, is very much our own position. Human pain and suffering may be nothing but the accompaniment of our own infancy, an essential of our being spiritual infants at all. In this childhood God may love us as a parent loves a toddler; but just as the exchange of human affection can become so much greater when children reach a stage of communion with their parents which extends to the understanding and hopes and ideals of later years, so we may perhaps accept (as we must, if we believe the teaching of Jesus) that the love of God for the individual extends far beyond the brief period of birth and adolescence, adulthood and death. The human parent loves his baby as a reflection of his own power of creation, but in doing so he looks ahead to the time when that love will be shared in maturer understanding. He loves his child not just for the past or for the fun of the moment, but for what it may one day become, and it is because of the forward-looking nature of his affection that he himself will readily accept any burden and even bear the temporary rebuffs of rebellion, confident that a future lies before his child. In somewhat the same way the love of God experienced in human life might well imply a future ahead. Of that future we can no more understand the circumstances or details than can new-born infants comprehend what it will be like to be grown-up, but at least we can see that Christian assertions on the matter of an " after-life " make sense, particularly in this matter of suffering.

It is important to realise that this is in no way a proof of an " after-life." That death is not necessarily the end is something which Christians merely accept from the authority of one whom they know and love and respect; but if experiences make sense within this item of belief and fail to do so outside it, then this is at least something in the nature of evidence to confirm the hypothesis taken on trust.

Without the assumption that our life on the Earth is no more than a preparation, a larval stage one might almost say, then I myself could not accept that the suffering of the innocent was at all in harmony with the belief in a God who loves not just mankind in general but *each* human individual, including the amaurotic and the mongoloid, here and now. The pain of the animal creation and of mankind may have been necessary for the emergence of man, and I believe that all our modern knowledge of evolutionary mechanisms demonstrates very clearly that this is the case, but the existence of humanity as an end-product might really reflect nothing more on the part of the creator than great ingenuity and virtuosity. The fact that men and women can live and move and have their being and even be aware of God does not automatically rule out selfishness on the part of the creator; and even if he cared for mankind as a whole he could conceivably show considerable callousness towards the individual. This would, I think, be the inescapable conclusion if we thought that no fulfilment but death and burial lay ahead of those whose lives on earth contain little, if any, possibility of their development as individuals capable of all that we regard as basic to human life. The infantile amaurotic idiot and the mongoloid, the schizophrenic and the hydrocephalic would then be no different from the animals—creatures who in their suffering carry part of the load of our own awareness, but who are not human. This might indeed be the case, but the attitude of Jesus towards the crippled and paralytic does not suggest that intelligence or lack of it was thought of by him as separating people into the class of proper potential humans on the one hand and mockeries of might-have-beens, with no more than a fleeting physiological function, on the other. If these, and all others whose life is hemmed in by restrictions of abnormal development or disease, are really within the love of a God who sustains the universe, then perhaps the truth may be that our own human life or larval stage carries more opportunity for development and response here and now than does theirs, but I cannot see that we have any reason to believe that as individuals they are just so much waste protein or that their maturity beyond this life is to be in any way less than our own. If, because they are as yet incomplete, they are fundamentally different from ourselves for ever, then either they are not human, or else God is indifferent to their suffering. The Christian asserts that God sustains the whole universe, mongoloids and imbeciles and all, and to me such a claim can only make sense within the concept that the railway track of birth and life and death is no more than the long or short platform from which the train sets out to its destination. And this, unless I am quite mistaken, is what Christ was continually telling people, and it is the belief in which millions throughout the ages have been prepared to die.

Nor need we feel that the idiot and imbecile or the child who dies at birth are necessarily at a disadvantage. One might almost suggest that they were at something of an advantage in having at least no need of forgiveness for evil choices which they have not had the opportunity to make.

CONSCIENCE AND FREE WILL

When a Christian talks of the moral law he is usually
thinking not just of an overall goodness permeating the
universe, but of something which is near enough at hand
to concern mankind in actual choice. Its relevance to
human affairs is something which is very real and involves
right and wrong in human action. To know what may be
right is not necessarily easy, but the deliberate choice of
what is believed or admitted to be wrong action is what
the Christian means by " sin." Sin always involves action,
even if it be the action of remaining passive towards the
sins of others, or doing nothing to satisfy their desperate
physical needs—a fact which, I think, is sometimes overlooked by those mystics who believe that mere intellectual
or spiritual acceptance of God in the seclusion of a college
court or a cathedral close or a desert cell is to have found
the truth.

I do not see how the existence of the moral law could
ever be demonstrated scientifically in the way that a
scientific hypothesis can be subjected to test. Indeed, we
should not really expect either the existence of such a law
or its detailed nature to be proved or disproved, for in itself
the moral law is not a cause of anything. It is obedience or
disobedience, according to the Christian, which may show
its effects in individual life or human history, rather than
the law itself.

The existence of the law is accepted or rejected as a
matter of belief. One may believe, for example, that it is
better to give than to receive or to love than to hate, and
the Christian says that these things are aspects of the moral
law which are immutable and unassailable, but there is no
possibility of proving by statistics or any other means that
loving is actually better than hating. Humanly speaking,

some of the world's greatest haters are very successful, but whether they are quite so successful in the sight of God may be a very different matter.

Of course the absence of scientific proof does not mean that a thing is improbable, and in the last resort scientific theories may be held on faith in very much the same way. A physicist who says that entropy always increases and goes on to forecast what will be the state of the solar system five hundred million years hence is in much the same position as the Christian who asserts that loving is better than hating (which he may not be able to check from his own experience). Both are expressing what they believe to be ultimate truths, and the chief difference lies in the authority behind their statements. The scientist derives his concept from observation, but the Christian does not. He asserts the existence of an absolute good and evil primarily on the authority of Christ, who clarified but pitched even higher the concepts of the Hebrews with regard to ultimate right and wrong which had become somewhat confused with priestly by-laws. He may even say that the course of history confirms what he believes, but he recognises that other different interpretations of human history could be put forward, as they frequently are—and very reasonably, too.

This moral law, the ultimate right and wrong, the Christian considers to be unalterable and emanating from God, and in this respect to be as much a property of the universe as are the relationships of energy which we can describe by such concepts as the laws of thermodynamics. But its mere existence involves man in response. Part of the uniqueness of man consists in this very ability to choose a course of action, and even denial of moral law does not conveniently rid him of having to make decisions of some kind. Animals do not appear to have this problem, for reflexes and instinctive behaviour patterns seem to control their lives from start to finish. Man has these forces in his make-up too, but the essential difference is that they do not necessarily have the last word in determining human behaviour. For example, a cat treading on hot bricks will immediately jump off them, but men are able to stretch their hands into the flames and be burned at the stake for their beliefs. It is not that the pain can somehow be wished away, but that the choice can be made deliberately, in frank opposition to the reflexes and protective mechanisms which are identical with those of the cat.

One of the greatest difficulties of the Christian, who cannot make or alter the rules to suit himself, is that the moral law in its entire application to human life is not easily transcribed. It is one thing to assert that there is an absolute moral law which is as much the sheer fabric of the universe as are the electrons and protons, but quite another to draw up a complete code of behaviour which divides everything neatly into what is known to be right and what is known to be wrong. Nor did Christ himself leave behind a detailed instruction manual of do's and don't's to cover every possible situation. He was content to point the direction of right action in general terms, in two precepts which he quoted from writings of the Old Testament, *"Thou shalt love the Lord thy God with all thy heart and strength"* and *"Thou shalt love thy neighbour as thyself."* This golden rule is as near as we can probably get to a summary of instructions for obedience to the moral law, and no system of philosophy has ever produced anything finer—or more exacting. Yet to interpret even this in terms of human actions and human choice is by no means as simple as one might think. The attitude of the individual towards war is an example, for where such an admitted evil as war exists (as the result of human offence against the moral law) Christians of undoubted sincerity take opposite views on the matter according to whether they think that to combat militant evil by fighting, or to abstain from slaughtering others whether guilty or innocent is more in line with the will of God.

Christians believe that man has freedom of choice in electing to do good or evil, and in considering how far this choice is really free we must see how it is made at all. There is tradition, and the experience of others, and there may be philosophical debate; but in the last resort there is the matter of conscience. Men and women (and not only

Christians) talk of "searching their consciences," but it would surely be a mistake to think of conscience as a telephone relay system through which one can dial GOD and get a report in the way one may dial TIM in London to hear the time. A decision may sincerely be a matter of conscientiously trying to do the will of God, but it may be a wrong one just the same.

It is not easy for Christians to admit that this can be so, but there can be no serious doubt about it. During the last quarter of the sixteenth century men and women of the Netherlands who read the Bible to themselves or their households were dragged out, tortured, flayed alive, or roasted over a slow fire. Those who treated them in this way for the offence of wanting to know more about their Lord were not Saracens or Melanesian head-hunters but *the agents of the Christian Church*. It is easy to say that the men of the Inquisition were bestial tyrants far removed from mere humanity, let alone from Christianity, but this does not fit the facts. Many of those who approved of such deeds and who personally organised and assisted at them, were men of undoubted sincerity who honestly believed that they were carrying out the will of God according to their consciences. I doubt if one could find a single Christian to-day, Catholic or Protestant, who would not agree that these acts were the most frightful offences against the law of God and the actual teaching of Jesus; and if these men could dial GOD through their consciences then they must have been connected with the wrong number—perhaps, as a Catholic once said to me, it was like telephoning in the dark and ringing SAT by mistake.

Even from this one instance it must be clear that conscience is not infallible. That the right is there to be discovered we must surely believe, and if it can be wrongly apprehended then we must seek an explanation. We cannot dismiss the phenomenon of the Inquisition as a mere historical relic, for we have no assurance that as members of the modern Church we may not be doing something very similar. Three hundred years from now it may well puzzle our successors when they read that hundreds of thousands of conscientious Christians of our own time really believed that the World Wars, however regrettable, were things which they had to accept and even take part in and were quite unable to stop.

I do not think Christians need necessarily be surprised if conscientious people make mistakes. They are, after all, as human as anyone else, and their decisions are made within a framework of knowledge and outlook which is extremely complex and is inevitably influenced by their upbringing, their surroundings, and their indoctrination (in both the good and the more familiar bad sense of the word). They are not judges set apart to view the world from some pure and lofty vantage point, but are involved in all the dealings of the world of humanity of which they are a part. And they are caught up in its evil, whether they like the fact or not. Not a single Christian in Britain or the United States or indeed in Europe can divest himself of all responsibility for the burning alive of thousands at Hiroshima; even if he was unaware of what was being planned (as nearly all of us were) he was part of the system of the civilisation which did the deed. This is part of what the Christian means when he talks of people being born into sin; if there is sin in human affairs then he is part of it, through no choice of his own, and if this were not the case it might be easier always to make correct decisions from conscience.

Whether we are all able to apprehend right and wrong to an equal extent is a very important question, and it is at this point that we have to consider what we know of the make-up of human personality. Our knowledge of human genetics is not perfect but at least we know beyond any doubt that the sorting which takes place in the course of forming the reproductive cells results in the ovum of a human mother being any one of 8,388,638 types (each of which is unique to her alone) and that the sex cells of the father are equal in their variety. The result is that each child is merely one out of more than 70 million million different children which it *might* have been—and actually this number would be considerably higher if we were to take into account the possibilities of crossing-over between chromosomes. Which combination of chromosomes each parent happens to provide at conception is nothing but chance, and the physical outfit of hereditary material which a child receives is absolutely random. And yet it is extremely important, for not only stature and shape and the fine details of anatomy and metabolism but also special aptitudes and intelligence are known to be greatly affected by which ticket is drawn in this astonishing genetical sweep-stake. That this gives plenty of scope for variety is true enough, but we are bound to concede that our own frame-work of mind and body is provided by an entirely random mechanism which includes some very poor endowments at one end of the scale and brilliant combinations of character-istics at the other. And the inheritance we thus receive will affect our whole lives in a very radical way. No amount of special schooling will turn a dull-witted child into a brilliant one, and we cannot escape the conclusion that such things as our appreciation of the real content of problems of conduct, and even our ability to respond with insight to the teachings of Jesus are determined at least in part by the lottery of the genes.

That mere intelligence may affect an individual's respon-sibility and hence the extent to which his will is really free to order his actions, is obvious enough. At the bottom end of the scale a person of very low intelligence may be much more driven by instinctive behaviour than others are, and when he appears before the magistrates on a charge of assault or violence he may say (quite truthfully in some cases) that he is sorry, but he was just " carried away " by an impulse. " Diminished responsibility," however difficult it may be to assess, is a concept in British law, and rightly so. As an extreme case we can take that of a patient in a mental institution in England who cut off the head of a neighbour-ing patient when he was asleep, and when asked why he did so explained that he wanted to see what the man said when he woke up and found his head was missing. Most of us act with more foresight than this, but few can foresee all the consequences of their actions in an exceedingly complex world, and those of not very great intelligence may be genuinely unable to look ahead to results which many others would consider quite obvious. Even the most conscientious people may choose a course of action which, because of their lack of understanding, can lead to results which cannot possibly be described as good.

Nor are our actions influenced only by the intellectual outfit handed us by heredity, for emotions can have a great effect upon our objectivity and colour our apprehension of what is right. These emotions may partly be determined by the genetical sweepstake, acting through over-development or irregularity of the endocrine organs which are responsible for controlling our sex and growth by discharging specific servo-chemicals into the bloodstream. That genes have a very marked effect in this way cannot be doubted, for the study of identical twins reared under different environments often reveals a surprising identity of reactions and habits and inclinations between members of a pair. Much of inborn personality can be directly related to the social effect of such mundane things as stature, and we are all familiar with the aggressiveness which so often accompanies smallness of build. Psychologists can give a very reasonable explanation of the relation between stature and confidence and attitude to others, but to a great extent the basis of sheer size and shape is purely genetic and random.

Quite apart from the hereditary lottery which fits us out with our intellect and with part of our emotions, there is the gamble of the environment into which we are born. Anyone who has worked in marriage guidance or with problems of human relationships knows the strong emotional characteristics which may come from being the only boy in a family which contains four or five elder sisters, or from being an only child, or the unwanted child of an unmarried mother. There are attitudes learned from others in childhood, too, and even the effects of accidents or sickness in the home, and the childhood fears which take root so strongly in the subconscious. And besides all this we are born by chance into a particular cultural background, the customs and traditions of which can be powerful in moulding our attitudes, as we can see from the varying dominant opinions in different parts of the world towards measures designed to give or withhold true equality of blacks and whites and coloured people. Even Christians of white race who confidently assert that all men are equal under God, and that there should be absolute freedom of opportunity, do not always find that they could contemplate their own daughters marrying coloured men.

Any faith that we might have had in the fundamental reliability and integrity of the ordinary human should long ago have been removed by the fearful spectacle of the effects of brain-washing in Communist countries, by which the most devoted and strong-minded individuals have sometimes been led to revile all that they formally held dearest on intellectual or religious grounds. Brain-washing is an extreme case, but the minds of all of us are subjected to some degree of soaping from the mere circumstances in which we happen to live, and the random influences of both heredity and environment go a long way to determining not just who we are, but how we react to a challenge of any kind—whether it be one of physical danger, or of selecting a course of action. It is not very surprising if efforts to interpret a moral law by conscience sometimes go astray when so many strange factors beyond our control are inherent in the relay system.

A Christian who is also a scientist might wonder whether the ability to be aware of God at all is genetically determined. This may at first seem rather a shocking suggestion, but knowing what we do of the heredity of mental abilities and special acuity of the senses it is at least worth considering. And if one holds that the real hall-mark of man as a species is his consciousness of God (in however primitive a form), then there can only be two possible explanations of how he came to be equipped with it during his emergence from the evolutionary past. Either it was genetic in origin, or it was planted, sown like a seed by divine intervention.

For myself, thinking of the universe as entirely within God rather than as a physical maze in which he can occasionally interfere, the former is much more acceptable. And if it should still seem rather strange to think of awareness of God as genetically determined, it is surely not unreasonable to think of the universe as teeming with a creative activity which only begins to take on its fullest meaning when matter can respond in love to its maker. For this to be possible at all a minimum highly complex organisation in terms of nerve cells and anatomy must be necessary; in other words, there can be no real awareness without a mind. Any biologist will agree that the mind of man, somehow connected with the organisation of his brain, is a product of evolution; and its emergence over ten million centuries of developing complexity from the first living types has been a process in which genetic variation undoubtedly played a very important part. In this sense one can hardly regard the awareness of God as anything other than genetic in origin, even if the genes were not dominants or recessives for holy and unholy, but were concerned entirely with emancipating the organism from physical inadequacy and allowing life to develop along the only channel in which its inherent godliness could at last find expression. I personally find such a concept in harmony with my own limited experience of the universe, and far more inspiring with awe and reverence than the alternative of special intervention and the implanting of a " soul."

But whether or not one agrees that awareness of God might have been genetic in origin, one may also consider whether this consciousness is present to an equal degree in every individual, or are there perhaps some who can hardly be aware of God at all? One might genuinely think that there is some complex Mendelian inheritance of God-consciousness or spiritual awareness, with greater or lesser conditions produced by enhancing genes. Before throwing out such a suggestion as fantastic we may recall that until recent times no one would have imagined that outstanding musical ability was a genetic endowment rather than something attained entirely by effort or by sheer interest in music, yet we now know very well that this is the case. Besides, it is not at all unreasonable to expect those genes which grossly affect the mentality to have some impact even on the most spiritual of human attributes. This is not to say that faith is a direct function of intellect; a single reading of any of the gospels is enough to show that Christ did not regard faith as a particular possession of any one level of intelligence. Yet just as our ability to distinguish between good and evil is not absolute but is influenced by so many factors behind the scenes, it is not impossible that our individual apprehension of God might be limited by similar circumstances, some of them genetic. However, I do not think we have any evidence on this point. That people respond in a very different degree, ranging from the atheist to the saint, is obvious enough, and it is equally clear that men of great intelligence and others of very simple mind can be deeply devoted to the service of God, or can flatly reject him outright, or may prefer, like most of us, to offer such limited devotion as does not interfere too much with other distractions. The Christian assertion is that *every* man is free and able to accept God or to reject him, and we do not have any warrant to except even the mongoloid idiot; his response might well take a form less easily visible, but we do not know that it does not exist.

However this may be, it is clear that the freedom of the human will is not absolute but is influenced by the many factors I have mentioned; and if it exists only within the limits set by a framework of culture, environment, subconscious, genetic outfitting and the rest, the question is whether this is the whole story and conscience is just an umbrella word to cover all these assorted tendencies and has no existence apart from them—whether in fact there is any freedom of will at all which is more than a reaction along predetermined lines. I think the answer is that we have very good reason to believe that there is something else, which can only be described as the direct response of the individual to the Holy Spirit. There are plenty of interesting cases, and none more dramatic than those of the young and admirably brain-washed young men carefully reared by the Nazis in a strict code of cruelty to their fellows, and installed as guards and executioners in concentration camps. That some of these when brought to trial expressed utter bewilderment on finding that there were people who considered their actions not only wrong but subhuman need not surprise us; what is much more instructive is the occasional case in which one of these highly-conditioned murderers would suddenly announce that what he was ordered to do was utterly wrong and he would not do it. To say this had only one result—the young man was promptly shot for his pains. That death was the punishment was clearly enough understood, but it did not deter such a man from defiantly taking his stand and electing to do what he " knew " was right.

We may well ask how he could suddenly unlearn all he had learned, and defy his superiors on the basis of a thing being evil. Was it just the heroism or resignation of his victims which softened him up? Or was it that the Holy Spirit could penetrate even the darkest corners of the mind of man? And if the latter, why did it only happen to some and not to others?

I doubt if we know the answer, but a Christian believes that no human mind is quite impervious to awareness of the Holy Spirit (or presence of God) and to apprehension of the moral law. This is another way of saying that no man is really *unable* to know that there are such things as good and evil—though whether or not he responds to such knowledge is a matter over which he himself has control through his free will. This freedom may be limited in its efficiency by brain-washing and environment and genes, but the rôle of these factors is not entirely over-riding. The freedom of some may be more easily exercised than that of others, but I do not think there is any evidence that there are any humans utterly impenetrable by the Holy Spirit, and thus robbed of every vestige of freedom of response. This seems to have been the view of Christ himself, and he indicated the very great but not absolute power of circumstances when he said that it was particularly hard for a rich man to enter the Kingdom of Heaven— a prerequisite of which was to do the will of God. But he did not say that there was any man who *could* not enter, provided he opened his heart to the challenge of God's presence.

I think we have to recognise that heredity and environment, acting in a somewhat rigid and capricious way, set the outer bounds within which an individual may develop a response to the will of God. Each of us is free to use his conscience—that is, to endeavour sincerely to apprehend for himself what is right within the limits of those boundaries. Certain complexities of human relationships or international affairs may lie beyond the fence for many of us and, like the men of the Inquisition, we may make mistakes when we are sincerely trying to extract by our own efforts courses of action which can only be determined if we are in possession of data lying beyond the fence. This is another way of saying that we cannot always be sure of doing right unaided. But the Christian doctrine of the nature of the relationship between man and God is that there is direct access, irrespective of class or colour or intellect or circumstances, and that man need never act entirely without aid. Often he will choose to do so, on the basis of his own interpretation of doctrine or tradition or Christian philosophy, and I suspect that this may have been what was wrong with the Inquisition. The men responsible may sincerely have thought that they were doing the will of God, but the bounds set by an inward-turning ecclesiastical tradition were set so close that they could not penetrate them unaided. A little more heart-searching meditation and prayer might have led to a course of action in which the love of God was more clearly revealed than the decisions of men, and the result might have been very different. This may also be true of much that we ourselves do in all sincerity, either as individual Christians or within the Church.

To say this suggests that by prayer one can overcome all the limiting circumstances and attain to the true will of God or ultimate right in every case. If this is really so, how can we account for the fact that extremely devout and prayerful Christians may come to opposite conclusions over such a matter as war? This enigma is, I think, one of the greatest which confronts all Christians, and I do not know that we can be sure of the answer. It is possible, however, that the absolute right in either case is really the same, and that it does not consist merely in fighting or not fighting but rather in the full determination to mediate to our neighbours as much of the love of·God as lies within our power. For some this might be expressed in defending their lives, and for others in serving them in needs of quite another kind. If, as I have suggested, our response is somewhat confined within bounds set by factors over which we ourselves have no control, then it is not at all impossible that the means of expression might differ from one person to another, and apparently conflicting actions might really reflects the will of God truly apprehended by individuals whose bounds were very differently set.

FAITH AND TRUTH

Although in one respect so simple that it can be grasped by the uneducated man or woman in the African bush or Indian plains or the back streets of Mile End and the Bronx, the Christian faith is one of the most complex things in human experience, and some of its foundations I have already mentioned. There are of course others, and if I have not looked at them here in any detail it is not because I think them any less important but because they do not seem to me to be points at which the modern scientific mode of thought makes any very special impact.

The gospels, the truth of which seems to me beyond all reasonable doubt, contain other concepts, too, on which I have not touched at all—angels, the devil, possession and the like. There is much to be said on all these subjects, and learned men have considered them for centuries; but I do not think that modern science gives any particular insights one way or the other.

I have made a passing reference to prayer, which is an absolute essential for the Christian if he believes (as he must) that God and man are in communication, but I have not attempted to analyse either the way in which an individual can open his heart and mind to God, nor how it may come about that the prayers of others (and even of those unknown to him) can bring real strength to an individual in need. As yet such sciences as parapsychology are only in their infancy and there is little data with which to compare the mass of Christian experience concerning prayer, but it seems at least possible that the day will soon come when new studies and new techniques will bring this activity within the bounds of investigation.

Then there is worship, with all that it involves not only in prayer but in praise and ritual and the sheer humble

" giving of glory " to God. And there is the Church in all its complexity of form, which to the Christian is not just a human society like a world-wide philosophical association or mutual assistance club, but is viewed as founded by authority and held to be a company which is somehow under the direct and special ownership of God, even if the officers and executives and workers on the production-line of the enterprise are only human. There is also the whole matter of the working of the Holy Spirit in history and in the life of the individual; and there is " the hope in the life to come." By the nature of these things they are far removed from scientific analysis, and I do not think that they raise different problems for the scientist than they do for others. Forgiveness, redemption, the sacraments, these too may be concepts essential to the Christian, but they are not ones for which scientific discoveries have any special relevance.

A glance even at the Apostles' Creed shows how little I have attempted to cover, and as the concepts dealt with in this book are marked in italics the very small proportion of the whole is only too obvious :—

I *believe in God the father almighty, maker of* heaven and *earth* : *and in Jesus Christ* his only son our lord, who was conceived by the Holy Ghost, born of the virgin Mary, *suffered* under Pontius Pilate, was crucified, dead, and buried, he descended into hell; the third day he *rose again from the dead,* he ascended into heaven, and sitteth on the right hand of God the father almighty; from thence he shall come to judge the quick and the dead.

I believe in the Holy Ghost; the holy catholic Church; the communion of saints; the forgiveness of *sins*; the resurrection of the body, and the life everlasting. Amen.

Amen indeed! And just what we really mean by " ascended into heaven " when we repeat the time-worn phrase in these days of a round Earth in a solar system which is no more than a fragment of the Milky Way, we may well ponder. Even if in our own minds we like to do a little autumn pruning of individual words here and there we are still left with more to *believe* than we can possibly comprehend through reason alone. But that is the essence of faith, and if in my own way I have attempted to discuss some of the aspects of Christian belief it is not because I have any feeling that faith as such is something dubious. On the contrary, even in human relationships faith in other people is essential, and every one of us accepts certain attributes of those we love as a matter of trust or faith rather than as intellectual propositions.

Sometimes, however, circumstances arise when what one discovers independently or from other sources may raise doubts in the mind. A young man who accepts implicitly that his girl loves him deeply may stumble on something which causes him to wonder if this is really the case. If he shuts his eyes and ears he may be making as great a mistake as if he accepts the wildest rumours without investigation. I think this is very much the position of the Christian in the age of science. His devotion may be reinforced by personal knowledge and a considerable amount of circumstantial evidence, but primarily it is one of trust. Any discoveries which might hint that things are not what he believes them to be should be taken as a challenge to examine the details and the grounds of his faith, and find out as far as he is able whether its essentials are shaken or reinforced.

I began this book by saying that a Christian has nothing to fear in facing truth, from whatever source it may come. For myself, I cannot pretend to solve all those mysteries which have confronted Christians for nearly two thousand years, but at least I can feel that science, as a revelation of part of the total truth, has often imbued certain elements of the Christian faith and doctrine with a grandeur and depth of meaning of which I would otherwise have been unaware. Here and there it has swept away the cobwebs spun by a few medieval spiders across the windows of human perception, but in doing so it has revealed more clearly the astounding beauty of the view beyond. And to me, this is the greatest gift which the astonishing growth of scientific knowledge can bring. I am grateful for drugs and brain surgery, for radio-communications and the prospect

that we may soon have cheap power without sending our
fellows down the colliery shafts; but most of all I am thankful for those discoveries which have thrown down a challenge to my belief and have forced me to scrutinise the
faith I have inherited and learned from others, and to
discover for myself that if it is weighed on the micro-
balance it is certainly not found wanting.

THE END

Other Fontana Religious Books

SCIENCE AND CHRISTIAN BELIEF

C. A. Coulson. The author sets out to show that, far from out-dating and nullifying traditional Christian beliefs, science is essentially a religious activity, playing its part in the unfolding of the nature and purpose of God.

THE MEANING OF PAUL FOR TO-DAY

C. H. Dodd. Professor Dodd suggests the place of Paul in the history of religion, and seeks to bring out the permanent significance of the apostle's thought, in modern terms, and in relation to the general interests and problems which occupy the mind of the present generation.

THE PERENNIAL PHILOSOPHY

Aldous Huxley. The author illustrates and develops passages from the writings of those Saints and Prophets from all monotheistic religions who have approached a direct spiritual knowledge of the Divine.

" A mine of curious and erudite learning."

New Statesman

CHRISTIANITY AND HISTORY

H. Butterfield. With force and profundity the author states his belief that history testifies to Christianity and Christianity interprets history.

THE JOURNALS OF KIERKEGAARD

Ed. Alexander Dru. A unique combination of notebook and diary in which Kierkegaard's spiritual and intellectual development are intimately recorded.

CHRISTIAN DOCTRINE

J. S. Whale. The author describes and meets the difficulties which the great Christian doctrines raise for us to-day, and shows how the Christian faith understands human history and death.

A SHORT BIBLE

Arranged by Austin Farrer. " I am more than pleased, I am excited, by Austin Farrer's book. I don't know that I ever learned so much (from anything of the same sort and on the same scale) as I have done from his introduction. This is a brilliant popularisation as we are ever likely to see."

C. S. Lewis

Other Fontana Religious Books

THE NEED TO BELIEVE

Murdo Ewen Macdonald. Relates the Christian message to the situation of modern man : believer and unbeliever alike.

THE PLAIN MAN'S BOOK OF PRAYERS

William Barclay. This book is written to help those who wish to pray. Dr. Barclay, distinguished scholar, gifted preacher, and regular broadcaster, has written this book specially for Fontana.

THE SCROLLS FROM THE DEAD SEA

Edmund Wilson. Writing with first hand knowledge the author's account of the discovery, unearthing and ultimate recognition of the Scrolls as priceless Biblical treasures is thrilling reading. Absorbing too are his own ideas on their value and his inquiry into the conflicting views of the experts still studying these remarkable documents.

ON THE EDGE OF THE PRIMEVAL FOREST

Albert Schweitzer. After renouncing his academic future in Europe to qualify as a doctor, the author whose personality is vividly reflected in his writings, describes the building and growth of his hospital at the edge of the damp, disease-ridden Equatorial forest of the Belgian Congo.

MORE FROM THE PRIMEVAL FOREST

Albert Schweitzer. An unadorned and poignant account of almost incredible difficulties and achievements, this book is based on reports sent home by Dr. Albert Schweitzer during his second period in Africa from 1924-27.

SEX, LOVE AND MARRIAGE

Roland H. Bainton. "Dr. Bainton lays before us the Christian attitude, past and present, to this important subject. He shows us how, amongst others, St. Augustine faced these problems and how it was as real to them as it is to us to-day. This is a book which no one can afford not to read."

THE PLAIN MAN LOOKS AT THE BIBLE

William Neil. This book is meant for the plain man who would like to know what to think about the Bible to-day. It deals with the relevance of the Bible and restates its message for the Twentieth Century.

NAUGHT FOR YOUR COMFORT

Trevor Huddleston. The author describes his twelve years ministry in Sophiatown, the coloured quarter outside Johannesburg from 1944-56. Father Huddleston has become world famous for his championship of the rights and dignity of the non-European races in South Africa.